Live The Life of Your Choice

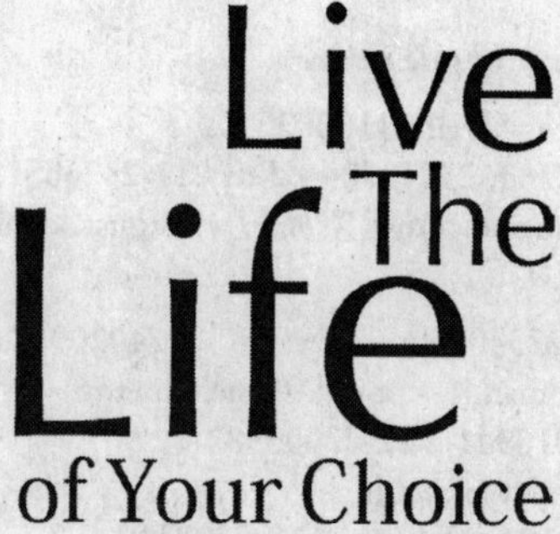

J.M. Mehta

Publishers
Pustak Mahal®

Administrative office and sale centre

J-3/16 , Daryaganj, New Delhi-110002
☎ 23276539, 23272783, 23272784 • *Fax:* 011-23260518
E-mail: info@pustakmahal.com • *Website:* www.pustakmahal.com

Branches
Bengaluru: ☎ 080-22234025 • *Telefax:* 080-22240209
E-mail: pustak@airtelmail.in • pustak@sancharnet.in
Mumbai: ☎ 022-22010941, 022-22053387
E-mail: rapidex@bom5.vsnl.net.in
Patna: ☎ 0612-3294193 • *Telefax:* 0612-2302719
E-mail: rapidexptn@rediffmail.com

ISBN 978-81-223-1412-0

Edition: 2013

Printed at : Param Offsetters, Okhla, Delhi

Dedicated to
my parents,
who taught me
how to live life.

Contents

Preface

Human life is a strange phenomenon of mysteries, ups and downs, pleasure and pain, joys and sorrows and similar other favourable and unfavourable experiences of varied nature. It portrays different forms and shapes to different people. All human beings differ from one another in some way or the other and no two human beings live life exactly in the same way. But two things are common to all beings, they are born one day and they have to die on another day. What happens in between these two days, makes different and strange stories.

Most human beings tread on the dotted lines, without knowing or even bothering to know about the art or manner of living life. They go on living, as if they are mere puppets in the hands of some mysterious great power, invisible but all-pervading and all powerful. In the words of Shakespeare, the great English poet and dramatist, we are just "Playthings of fate". One may or may not wholly agree with this statement. However, in general, life for an average person is not a very desirable state of living, considering that human species is on the top of all creation. It is therefore, extremely essential to know how to live life, which is an extraordinary opportunity for a person to make the best possible use of it.

As all human beings differ from one another, they live their life in different ways, depending upon their intrinsic attitudes, qualities and external influences etc. Broadly speaking there are three MAIN OPTIONS to live life. First is the MATERIAL PATH which most humans beings follow to experience the dualities of life. As this path is a strange mix of pleasure and pain, it does not provide full satisfaction or total happiness that one is looking for. Consequently, one is always hoping for a better and happier alternative, and therefore turns towards the SPIRITUAL PATH. According to our ancient scriptures and the experiences gained by various holy men, saints and seers, this is the only path which can lead to total happiness or eternal bliss, which is the highest attainment of human life. This path involves total dedication and devotion, complete commitment to righteousness and observance of strict spiritual discipline. Most people find this way of life extremely difficult and therefore only a rare few tread this path and live life accordingly. An average person remains ever dissatisfied and still gropes in ignorance not knowing, which way to go! In these circumstance for the vast majority, a ray of hope lies in following what may be called as the MIDDLE PATH, which is a mix of both the material and the spiritual ways of life. In this path, while enjoying the pleasure and pain of material life one tries to make gradual progress on the road to spirituality.

This small book deals with the three main paths to live life and briefly describes their pros and cons. Some helpful hints to live life in a desirable and righteous manner are also mentioned for the readers. There are Three Main Options to live life, it is for the reader to make an appropriate choice!

J.M. Mehta
J-186, Saket
New Delhi-110017
Tel. No.: 29555053

Understanding Human Life

Before we ponder over 'How to LIVE LIFE?' and make a choice, it is essential to know and understand human life and its significance. Most of us do not really know the importance of human life. We just go on living – from moment to moment, day to day and year to year till the end. We pass through periods of infancy and childhood, adolescence, youth and slowly the decline begins, and we slip into old age to perish at last. For an average person, life is a short span between birth and death.

The above description of life is only a short-sighted view and does not really convey the real picture. Human life is not just one span of a few years; this span is only an only intermediate stop of life is the long ever going Journey of numerous lives. This view is supported by the testimony of our holy scriptures. The *Bhagwad Gita* tells us that there was life before our present birth and it also continues after the event of death. It continues in different forms and death in our present state of existence is not the finial destination. In this context, verse 12 chapter 11 of the GITA is quoted as follows:-

> *'Never was there a time, when I was not, nor thou, nor these lords of men, nor there ever be a time hereafter, when we will all cease to be.'*

[Verse 12 .Chapter 11]

The above verse clearly corroborates that life is perpetual and continues for ever.

Speaking broadly, life is a combination of body, which is matter and soul - the conscious life element. Soul being a subtle entity can not function by itself and therefore needs a material structure and mechanism through which it can perform its functions. The physical framework, called the body acts as a medium through which the soul operates. This physical body has its instruments which inter-alia include the senses, the mind and intelligence etc. Thus the mutual cooperation of the body and the soul is essential for performing all actions in human life. While the body acts as the medium, the real master is the life element, or the individual self, called the soul.

The body is physical and thus visible. It may be easily understood and described. On the other hand, it is extremely difficult to understand and describe the soul which is not visible. Its existence can not be testified in any physical scientific laboratory. We have to believe it and analyse its existence and functioning on the basis of evidence furnished by holy scriptures. The Bhagwad Gita differentiates between the body and the soul in the verse quoted as follows:-

> *'The soul is never born, nor does it die at any time. It is unborn eternal, permanent and primeval. It is not slain when the body is slain'.*
>
> [Verse 20. Chapter 11]

The physical body is mortal while the soul is eternal. The Bhagwad Gita quotes a number of verses to distinguish between the body and the soul. The soul is the driving force of human life and never dies, it is the body or the physical framework which perishes. After death the soul takes on another body and the life moves on continuously from one span to another.

The short preview of human life given above is only indicative and not exhaustive. In spite of this brief and elementary description of life most individuals often wonder and say 'What is life.' It is extremely difficult to fully answer this question. Numerous people including philosophers, religious teachers, poets and writers have expressed different views, in this matter. Some of these views may be summarized as follows:-

Life is a short span between birth and death. Life is a DREAM! Yes it looks like so. In dreams we see something which fades away as soon as we wake up. In real life, what had happened earlier, no longer exists. Past life only remains in memories, like a dream.

"We are such stuff as dreams are made on; and our little life". That is what, the world renowned English dramatist and writer Shakespeare said in one of his plays.

Life is a BATTLE – Everyday we fight against odds. It is a battle between good and evil, right and wrong, pain and pleasure, against social customs and traditions.

Life is nothingness (मिथ्या) – It does not exist after one expires. Nay; it continues in another form.

Life is a MYSTERY–We do not know the purpose of our birth. Why someone is born rich and someone poor. Strange things happen which are beyond explanation. It is full of surprises and it is indeed a great mystery!

Life is a bundle of EXPERIENCES, incidents and events, happenings etc. It is a sum total of good or bad experiences.

Life is ACTION as non-action is death. Only a living person can do something, a dead person is incapable of doing anything. There is no life without action.

Life is a LEARNING process. A newly born child starts learning soon after birth. From birth to death is a learning process.

Life is a MISSION – a problem solving mission. We face problems and look for solutions everyday. These are problems of feeding, of health, of education, of profession, of children, etc. At every step, there seems some problem. That is why it is said life is of problem.

Life is the BEST SCHOOL, a great TEACHER. We learn many things from our daily experiences, we can not learn from books or schools.

Life is a JOURNEY, which starts right from birth and then continues till death. Even after death it continues in another shape. It seems an endless journey from one life to another, passing through different stops and stages.

Besides above descriptions, we can depict life as rosy, joy, fun, play, pleasure and pain, as misery, as duty or beauty and so on. It has so many aspects, that it is perhaps difficult to describe all. In short, it may be said that human life is a very COMPLEX PHENOMENON. Life is a Journey, is one of the most appropriate and short description of life. Now every journey has a goal as we have to reach a destination. It is said that life should have a goal, a purpose to achieve.

ROCKFELLER the world renowned industrialist of the U.S.A had observed on the purpose of life as follows:-

'The real purpose of our existence is not to make a living but to make a life'

It indicates that life is not meant just for eating or making money, it surely has a higher purpose, a final goal. Mere living is nothing, but right living is something. Human life is a rare opportunity to bring about the highest improvement in our life. Normally, life can be lived at the following three broad levels:-

I. **Animal level** – To satisfy hunger, desire etc. An animal eats, sleeps and procreates and lives on.

II. **Mental level** – It involves discretion; the discrimination between good and bad, right and wrong etc. One can make a choice, argue and analyse etc.

III. **Spiritual level** – It involves godliness, coming close to God. By following proper disciplines, one can attain the highest goal of life.

It has been mentioned earlier that life is a long journey which has four stages. These include birth, development, decline and distinctions. A child is born as a tiny infant, he enters his childhood which lasts for a few years and then marches to become a full-fledged young adult when he gets married, is blessed with children, follows a profession, lives life of a householder, earns wealth and material possessions, name and fame and other good things of life. After a few more years, the youthful years come to an end and life follows a path of decline when the period of post-retirement starts. Finally the flame of life gets extinguished when the final stage of death is reached. But death does not put a full stop to life which continues further after death, in the form of another Journey of life in another shape. Our scriptures describe the four stages of life in the form of FOUR ASHRAMS or SPANS OF LIFE. These are very briefly mentioned below:-

Brahmacharya – Period of first 25 years which lays down the foundation of life.

Grihastha – It involves married life of a householder – following a profession, raising a family and fulfilling mundane desires, etc.

Vanprastha – It is the stage of withdrawal from family life.

Sanyasa – It is the last segment of life when an individual lives a life of renunciation and aspires to achieve the final goal of life.

This arrangement to live life in an orderly and purposeful manner is an ideal way to live life. However in the present modern world of complexities and temptations, this system might not be feasible enough for most people. Only a few truly enlightened persons well-versed in ancient philosophy and culture may venture to opt for this system which is known as ASHRAM VYAVASTHA (Four spans of human life).

As mentioned earlier life is like a long journey. Every journey has a destination, a goal. The question arises, what is the goal of human life? As the life proceeds on its path, various small goals crop up and these goals keep on changing, according to our needs. Getting some education and preparing for a profession to earn livelihood becomes the main goal of a growing person. Then marriage and children is another concern. Gaining wealth, good health and material possessions are also the major goals of life besides several other connected goals. Behind all these smaller goals, the chief goal of life is to live in happiness. Thus happiness, in different forms is the chief and common goal of all humans. But it is observed that material happiness does not last for ever. It is short lived. All pleasures of life are of transitory nature, these come and go. There is also pain mixed with these pleasures. That is why the great GURU NANAK has said, 'The whole world is full of misery.' Consequently such a state of journey of life can not be construed as the real goal of life - the ultimate destination of human journey. Then let us consider, what is the ultimate goal of human life.

Our holy scriptures declare that God-realisation is the ultimate goal of life. When we are hungry, we go to the source of food. When we are thirsty, we seek the source of water. Similarly for other comforts, joy and material happiness we look for the means and the sources of pleasure, comfort and happiness. Obviously, for attaining ever-lasting happiness we should go to the source of such happiness. That source of eternal happiness is GOD, the creator of universe, the SUPREME BEING, who is the source of eternal bliss, SAT CHIT ANANDA.

That is why GOD realization is the main and the ultimate goal of human life. This goal can also be described in different ways. It may be called as the highest stage of perfection, the greatest peace (ANANDA) freedom from all sorrows or evils, freedom from bondage, liberation of the soul, purity of the Absolute, the latitude of GOD, THE SALVATION or MOKSHA or in some other similar ways. All these indicate towards the conclusion. The goal of life, therefore, he summed up as GOD - realization, which is the highest stage of spiritual attainment, beyond which these remains nothing else to be attained.

Having understood life and its various nuances, one would naturally like to know – 'How to live life'? It is the most vital question which every human being should ponder over and workout a plan or path to follow and achieve the desired end. In general every individual may like to chalk out his own path and live accordingly and that is what is happening in the real world, at present. Taking into consideration all these different ways, complexities of life and the chief goal of human life we may conclude that there are three main paths to live life:-

– The Material Path.

– The Spiritual Path.

– The Middle Path.

An individual may like to select one of these paths according to his inclination, mental make-up and other qualities of head and heart.

Influence of Three Modes (Gunas) on Human Life

In common parlance nature (Prakriti) is synonymous with matter. According to ancient Indian philosophy, nature is the material cause of all creation. Such as mind, body, senses and intelligence are evolutes of nature. In essence, nature comprises these modes (or Gunas) which are, SATTAVA, RAJAS and TAMAS. These gunas are the basis of all substances. All human activities are influenced by these gunas. The word guna implies the attitude, quality or tendency or the condition in which mind functions. These guans are co-existent and are inherent in varying degrees and thus determine their character and activities. The soul in the individual comes under the influence of these gunas and thus gets bound in the body. No body is free from these three gunas but in each being one guna may dominate over the remaining two. Accordingly, the character and activities of a particular individual are greatly influenced by the guna which is predominant. However the normal flow of human life starting from TAMAS tries to progress towards SATTAVA, the best of the three gunas.

As these three modes to nature are a major factor in determining the path which human beings follow in their lives we shall try to describe them briefly, as follows:-

Sattava– It stands for goodness. It reflects the light of consciousness and represents purity and luminosity. When this guna is in a dominant position it brings knowledge, peace and happiness in an individual. It's dominance has an inspiring purifying and creative influence on the mind. The SATVIK people like pure foods which help to increase vitality, joy and cheerfulness. Such foods are palatable, pleasant and their procurement is by non-violent means. Mainly vegetables, fruits, milk, products, nuts and pulses etc come under this category. The fruits of satvik actions are good, pure and pleasant. After death, satvik people are born at higher levels of mankind. Sattava, being pure, illuminating and blameless becomes the cause of binding the soul to happiness and knowledge. It creates attachment to happiness. When the light of knowledge sprouts through the body, it is the sign of the growth of sattava. The result of the noble actions of sattava is purity.

Rajas – It is in the nature of passion and is born out of attachment and desire. Passions form the salient features of a Rajsik individual and express themselves in different forms of desire, emotions, feelings etc. This mode has onward movement and binds the soul with actions connected with the external world. When RAJAS is dominant in an individual, selfish motives and action, greed, restlessness, craving for pleasures, etc are generated. It prompts material activity and produces desires for acquisition of material possessions and looks for situations which yield temporary pleasures and comforts and continuous attachment with them. Such a person is ever engaged in earning and spending, procuring and preserving and always desiring for more and more. He is always agitated and entangled in the Joy of his success and displeased at his failures. The fruit of rajsik actions are miserable. Their mind remains agitated and without peace. Rajsik people after death are re-born as men of selfish motives and desires. Rajas represents passionate nature, causes thirst and attachment and thus binds the soul to desire and action. After death Rajsik people take birth among those who are obsessed by activity.

Tamas – This guna is the source of ignorance and creates delusion. It binds the soul with indulgence, lethargy, sleep and creates dullness. When tamas is dominant in a person, he loses discrimination of right and wrong. He becomes slave to its lower nature and indolence. This guna makes a person devoid of noble thoughts and actions. The fruits of tamsik actions are ignorance. After death, such people sink to the lowest levels of existence.

As mentioned earlier these gunas are present in beings in different degrees. Thus individuals are Satvik, Rajsik and Tamsik on the basis of the particular guna which is dominant or prevails over the other two. When sattava is predominant, knowledge, peace and discernment rule over mind. When Rajas prevails greed, selfishness, activity and desires overcome and when Tamas dominates, ignorance, delusion and indolence overpower.

When the individual soul comes under the influence of gunas, it forgets its real self and uses body, senses and mind for temporary satisfaction and pleasures, which are binding and enslave the soul. When the soul by virtue of spiritual discipline rises above these modes of nature it gets liberated and attains the highest stage.

After having understood the role of three gunas a wise person shall surely try to inculcate satvik guna in his life. In this way he can overcome his influence of Rajas and Tamas. By developing the element of sattava gradually through long practice one can transcend these gunas and reach the perfect stage of eternal life.

Since these gunas have a powerful influence over the human mind, they play an effective role in determining the particular path an individual follows to live life. We shall now describe the three main paths to live life, in the following chapters.

The Material Path

We have already discussed the three main paths to live life. To start with, we shall deal with the material path first.

Material path is the most popular of all paths as it is full of temptations. It is being followed by most human beings. It seems that it is based on the premise that there is only one life so the best use of it should be made for gaining success, wealth, power, status, honour, name and fame so that one may live well and happy.

In this path, therefore all efforts are made to secure wealth which is the means to procure material possessions that can bring various comforts of life. Having amassed plenty of wealth, one can buy good food to eat well, a grand mansion to live, a big car to travel, all sorts of fashionable clothes and jewellery to wear and can also travel to beautiful places besides numerous other means of comfort, enjoyment and mundane pleasures. Enjoyment of life to its full becomes the main aim of material life. EAT, DRINK and be MERRY is the motto of material life. This way of life has great attraction for most individuals who are always running around and struggling to meet their material requirements according to their unlimited desires. Prima facie there seems nothing wrong in following the material path as every body has to eat and drink to enjoy and be merry. We have to eat and drink and be merry so that we may live our life happily. What really matters is – what we eat how we eat and why we eat. In following the motto 'eat drink and be merry,' we often forget to observe these basic principles and then come to harm instead of happiness.

Roti, Kapda aur Makan (Food, Dress and Housing)

The above three things are the fundamental requirements to live life.

Roti (Food) is utmost essential to nourish the body and for its physical and mental growth and development. Home food which is prepared from common vegetables and other such food elements under the supervision of a loving mother and wife, under hygienic conditions, accompanied by sweet feelings of love and purity is the best. But in the ever-changing pursuits of material life, we have made a vicious mess of the concept of simple home food. Instead of simple nourishing roti (or rice etc) we crave for rich, oily tasty prathas, puris, samosas and such other fried varieties along with sweets and junk foods. While tasty foods are not a taboo and may be taken once in a while for a change, these should be exception and as not the daily routine. Similarly in case of drinks, pure water, milk and natural juices are the best source for nourishment and good health and hence for good life. In this area too, man has invented a hoard of artificial and intoxicating drinks with a variety of tempting flavours and tastes. Alcoholic drinks are the worst forms of human ingenuity, besides aeriated artificial drinks and colas. These drinks are harmful and lead to addictions. It is often noted that alcoholic drinks, smoking and other intoxicating drugs etc. lead to harmful diseases like cancer, heart problems and so on. These are also causes of violence, theft, robbery, rapes and other unsocial activities which ruin numerous lives every day. In this manner, food (which includes drinks also) instead of being a potent source of happy and healthy life becomes a dangerous element for ruin and destruction.

As said earlier home food is the best. But people now are becoming increasingly fond of fast foods available outside home or in restaurants and hotels, malls etc. Children and younger people who remain outside most of the time fall ready victims to this type of outside food.

Such foods are generally fried, spicy, mixed with artificial mouth-watering flavours are becoming very popular with younger generation and other taste-hungry, ready to eat type adults. That is why the number of restaurants, shops, malls etc. which cater and supply such ready made stuff are ever increasing. But in our material way of life, not many people pay attention to the fact that the number of sick people and diseases resulting from eating such foods is also increasing. In the process of satisfying our taste buds we often indulge in over-eating which is a common cause of obesity and allied ailments. It has been observed that more people die due to overeating and excess of drinking etc. than due to hunger and lack of food.

Let us now ponder over the second most important need of material life. Dress is essential to cover the delicate human body. While animals do not need any clothing or dress as they have natural skin to take care of their need. But it is not so with human beings as their skin is quite delicate and is not a sufficient safeguard from the harsh realities of climatic factors and external environment. All that humans need is suitable clothing material which can be made from natural sources, such as cotton, wool and some similar other natural material. Here again man has invented and manufactured several products made from artificial sources, chemicals, animal skins etc.

Cotton and wool and in some cases leather (procured from dead animals) are the best sources for human dress. Silk is not considered desirable as it is prepared by non-violent methods after killing millions of silk-worms. But in material life, it is not only expensive but also much in demand.

Dress which is primarily necessary to cover human body for its protection and safety has become a symbol of modern fashion and an object of ostentation and false pride both of which are harmful for life. It is alright if one wears good dress which is of good quality, colour and adds to good looks etc. but there is hardly any necessity to wear clothes which are heavily embroidered, prepared by very expensive fashion designers etc. just to show off ones wealth. But this is often seen in the material way of life where dresses worth lakhs of rupees are worn, just for once in life and then are discarded and kept in a suitcase or dumped in an almirah.

Ornamental jewellery and precious stones and diamonds etc have also become part of dress, especially in case of ladies, in the material way of life. All this is a way of display of wealth and is wrongly considered a symbol of status in society. There is a saying "Beauty needs no ornaments." According to another saying "Handsome is he, who handsome does." The true beauty and the real worth of a person, lady or gentleman, lies in his or her good conduct. A person is well-dressed if he or she wears pleasing manners and displays good moral conduct even though their dress is simple and natural. Besides dress and jewellery, lakhs of rupees are wasted on the celebrations of marriages, birthdays and wedding days and similar other so called social parties where display of wealth is paraded in a naked fashion. These are only a few glaring examples of display of wealth, ostentation and false pride and many more are available in the every day conduct of material way of life.

Housing is the third most important necessity of material way of life. One needs a place to live and a roof over one's head. A single individual may need a smaller house and as he gets married and raises a family, the need for a bigger house arises. Then there is need for individual separate rooms, kitchen and bath room and so on. There is also need for furniture, utensils, bed material, electrical gadgets and other objects. Our ancient rishis used to live in simple huts with minimum objects. Their dress and food were very simple and were kept to the minimum. In modern times, the need for housing and its household items which include T.V., refrigerator, washing machine, cooking range and other electrical items etc. is becoming greater day by day. One is now unsatisfied with one or two bed rooms. There should be another rooms for guests and separate rooms for growing kids. Several storied houses have taken the place of a single storey house. The need for more and more accommodation is increasing with growing population. Small towns are becoming cities and cities are becoming bigger and occupying more space. More the population, more is the need for housing and its requirements. Cities are becoming narrower while their requirements and expanding. We need more water more electricity, more transport, more schools, colleges and hospitals etc. The demand is ever-increasing and seems endless, while resources do not seem to fulfill all these requirements and thus problems of every day life are increasing day by day. This situation puts lot of physical and mental strain upon human beings who are becoming victims of new diseases which were not visible in olden days. Human life for vast multitude is becoming unpleasant and in most cases unbearable. Crime situation is also getting worse.

The daily newspapers are full of increasing number of stories of crime, thefts, robberies, rapes and murders besides economic crimes, corruption, kidnaps and similar other unsocial criminal happenings. All these and many other adversities of human life are outcome of complexities and consequence of material way of life.

We have earlier briefly mentioned about the powerful influence of three modes of nature (gunas) upon human life. It is the RAJAS mode of nature which is at the back of all these complexities and adversities of material path of life. The nature of passion born out of attachment to material objects, persons and comforts etc. gives rise to greed, desires, strong emotions and feelings resulting in complex situations and adverse consequences. The interplay of rajas always creates endless activity, selfish motives, restlessness, craving for more and more possessions and pleasures of life which ultimately produce misery. Consequently, fulfillment of various desires becomes the main function of material path of life.

We shall now consider the role of desires in the material path.

Role of Desires in Material Path

Who does not have desires?

Most individuals and perhaps all individuals do have desires which may be of different types, nature and intensity. There is hardly any body who is free from desires. Even saints, holy persons who may not be having any material desire, must be having some desires of spiritual nature. They may be having an intense desire for God-realization. Some desires, such as for food, sleep and happiness are normal for all beings. However, in material path, these may be endless desires of varying degree and intensity. The objects of desire in this path inter-alia, include good health, wealth, material possessions, good wife, children, good career, high status, social and political power and so on. This list is not exhaustive and more may be added to it.

For any human being, some desires are fundamental and hence natural and essential. Every one desires to have food, rest and relaxation and good life in general. Success in all aspects of human life is a common desire. Besides all these, all beings would like to remain happy in life.

Desires act as catalytic agent for action in material path of living. If a person desires food, he will go out and look for some eating material. The human initially used fruits grown on trees and roots grown underground for eating. Their desire to eat different types of foods led them to grow plants and vegetables, etc. Eating and producing a variety of food items has been an ever-increasing desire of mankind.

The pursuit of human desire has resulted in countless inventions, discoveries and achievements which have led to tremendous material progress. As a result of success in the fulfillment of these desires, man can now fly in the air like a bird, run on the ground (in train etc.) like a tiger or even more than the fastest animal in the world, and swim in the ocean better and faster than a fish. With modern scientific machines and instruments, man has also landed on the moon. Many more achievements are yet to come.

The Gita tells us about the source of human desire as in the following verse:-

> *'When a man dwells in his mind on the objects of sense, attachment to them is produced. From attachment springs desire ......'*

[Verse 62 . Chapter 11.]

It is clear from the above verse that attachment to objects of the external world is the source of desires and this attachment is produced when mind through senses comes in contact with them and concentrates on them. When we see an object and think about it closely and constantly, attachment is produced. The intensity of attachment produces a desire to possess or enjoy or use that object in some way or the other. A desire is therefore a passionate feeling born out of attachment to a sure object. For an example if we see a beautiful flower in a public garden we would like to touch it, smell it or even pluck it. Due to the same reason, shops and commercial houses display their products in a beautiful manner in their show cases in big hoardings, in news papers, posters, T.V. etc and other means of media. Children get tempted to smoking when they see their popular film star smoking with a style on the T. V. screen on in a cinema house, etc.

In material way of life, desires in some form or the other are being produced constantly in the mind of every individual. A small child gets attracted towards most objects in the household, toys, butterflies, flowers even cats and dogs and so on. A young man gets attracted towards foods, fads, beautiful girls, dress and so on. This attraction or attachment produces desire to see, touch or possess a particular object. Thus desires continue to come throughout life and their flow, more or less is endless. This interplay of unending desires creates a world of what is commonly knows as MAYA JAAL and this play of desires ends only with the end of existence.

It is generally observed that desires are insatiable and one desire may lead to another and more and more. If one desire of a person is satisfied, the urge to satisfy another crops up. The tragedy of the material way of life is that most human beings spend their lifetime in the fulfilment of their mundane desires. They feel happy if a desires gets fulfilled and are found miserable if it is not. This vicious circle of human desire sometime leads to happiness and sometimes misery and pain, and this is how the journey of material life goes on. Since all desires are never met, an individual never feels satisfied and remains under stress and strain. When a person gets entangled in the vicious web of desires, most of which are never satisfied, he loses his peace of mind and thus ruins his life.

Desire is never satesfied by the enjoyment of the object of desire. Several examples of this nature are observed in the sphere of desire for wealth, possessions, food, and drinks, dress, jewellery, power politics, etc. The craze for new foods, new fashions more power and omnipotence etc is ever on the increase and it appears that this hunger will never be satisfied. Like fire to which fuel is added the desire grows more and more with enjoyment and indulgence. The desire for delicious foods, drinks, drugs, sexual gratification, wealth, property, status etc are some of the glaring examples. All desires which when become unlimited must he abandoned. Freedom from all selfish material desires leads to eternal peace.

Let us now consider how we should deal with desires in material way of life on day to day basis. In our daily life one should start with restricting desires to the level of necessities. One should not expand the list of desires and attend to only those which have to be satisfied as a mater of duty. As a general rule, all cravings and unnecessary desires leading to wasteful expenditure and undue harm must be curbed in the very beginning. As all desires originate in the mind it is in the mind that necessary control has to be exercised. One must examine and analyse the pros and cons before acting upon any material desire. One must ponder over the impending dangers which lurk in desires and consequently must reject evil or negative desires at the very start. It is easier to nip the evil in the bud. The fire of desire if controlled in the initial stage will not grow into big blaze which becomes difficult to extinguish later.

Firm mental discipline is very essential in curbing unnecessary desires. One must not yield to his evil tendencies. Again satisfaction of desires in the hope of getting rid of them will not end desires. However, the undue and forced suppression of desires is also not the right way to deal with them. Desires when forcibly suppressed are bound to roll back with equal force or even greater strength. One should therefore exercise gradual firm control rather than suppress or satisfy them. The solution lies in correct thinking and proper understanding of evil consequences of these desires. Strong determination and repeated reasoning and reminders are helpful in curbing harmful selfish material desires. Right approach and constant practice will help. Never lose patience as this is a very difficult process. Remember the proverb – slow and steady wins the race.

Desires play a significant role in our daily life. Take the example of our desires to eat spicy, sweet foods or ice cream and chocolate etc, because we like their taste. When you eat these for the first time and like the taste, you will have a desire to eat the same stuff again and again. When it becomes a habit and you develop an addiction for such stuff it can lead to health problems of indigestion, etc. Similarly one can develop a strong liking for other items which include food, drinks, smoking, money, dress material, sex, seeing films etc. One may also cultivate strong desire for name, fame, power, status etc. So long desires are legitimate requirement and are contained within proper limits, it is all right but when these take the form of a craze or strong addiction and go beyond the desirable limit, serious problems are bound to arise. Bad habits of chain smoking and drinking of liquor and addiction to drugs are some of the glaring examples of uncontrolled desires.

A desire is caused because there is something to seek, to acquire, to use from some external source. Generally we seek comfort and pleasure which is to our like. But when a desire becomes source of greed, it leads to disappointment and anger if it is not satisfied. Desires of material way of life often become a barrier which separates man from moral values, spirituality and the SUPREME. Therefore all desires should be cut down, reduced or eliminated altogether; if this is possible to do so. This would be possible if we regularly watch our thoughts, distinguish between good and bad, right and wrong and with the help of wisdom, exercise proper control over our senses and the mind. The best way to curb desires is to divert them to some other useful activity and to divert our attention from material desires to divine desire. The proper solution lies in curbing the desire from the very beginning. Nip the evil in the bud so that it can not grow further and create difficult situation.

As mentioned in the GITA, desire is a constant foe of the wise, sinful destroyer of wisdom and discrimination, the enemy within and is hard to overcome. As the maternal way of life is full of all sorts of desires it is not a suitable way to follow as it leads to evil consequences. In order to curb desires a step by step approach to raise the level of our awareness is necessary. We have to transcend the level of senses and mind and seek the help and guidance of the SUPREME. The important point in our daily life to practice should be – Do not let desires rule your life.

Pleasure and Pain in Material Path

In the material way of life, pleasure and pain go together or side by side or follow each other. Pleasure and pain are sisters twain. Human life consists of pleasant and unpleasant day to day experiences. While pleasant experiences give pleasure, comfort and happiness, the unpleasant ones leads to pain and misery.

Thus pleasure and pain are two sides of the same coin of life. The material path is full of both these elements.

It is an admitted fact that where there is pleasure, there is bound to be pain also. Sometimes pleasure leads to pain and these may be pleasure after pain. There is pleasure in attending a nice gala party or a marriage celebration where one eats delicious foods in excess because of their tempting taste and then falls seriously ill and suffers pain and misery. A pleasant Journey to a tourist place can end in some unpleasant situation. A healthy and beneficial friendship can end in an unhealthy and painful situation. A happy marriage can lead to an unhappy ending of divorce. A seemingly successfull attempt can end in failure. Our efforts and expectations do not always bring joy and pleasure. There are so many happenings and incidents which occur in life in this manner.

These are only a few examples and such examples can be multiplied from our every day material life.

The GITA explains the cause and nature of both these situations and also gives instructions to deal with them as indicated in the following verse:-

'CONTACTS with other objects give rise to cold and heat, pleasure and pain. These come and go and do not last for ever, learn to endure these.'

[Verse 14 - Chapter 11]

Our Joys and sorrows, pleasant and unpleasant experiences arise out of our numerous activities in our material life. We experience pleasure and pain when our senses come in contact with the objects or situations of the external world, either at home or outside. At home we may feel pleased and happy if good nice food is served, children obey our command, the housewife is always smiling and sweet-tempered and so on. And we shall be displeased, unhappy and in pain if the reverse of these situations happens. Similar is the case outside home. Thus our material life itself provides various opportunities and occasions for pleasure and pain. We feel pleasure if happenings are according to our liking and pain if these are adverse. This happens throughout human life. So long as we live, we have to face both these situations. The quantum of pleasure or pain may differ in different cases. Some may have more pleasure and less pain while others may have more pain than pleasure. It may be concluded that both pleasure and pain are unavoidable in life. Now how should we deal with these situations. The GITA tells us how to deal with these happenings as indicated in verse 14 Chapter 11. The solution lies in the last sentence of this verse, which clearly instructs– 'LEARN TO ENDURE'. These situations are bound to come. Therefore there is no option but to face and endure them as long as they exist. We must, therefore, exercise patience, learn how to face their challenges with calm composure and bear them with serenity of mind knowing fully well that these situations are bound to pass away. We should meet such situations with evenness of mind. In our moment of happiness and pleasure, we should not get over excited and start jumping with joy and making all sorts of unnecessary noises. Similarly in moments of pain and grief one should not feel utterly miserable, aggrieved or disturbed. Equanimity of mind must be maintained in both cases. In real life situations this may not be easy to practice. A correct understanding and constant practice of endurance will be helpful.

Let us now consider some examples from everyday life in the material path of living. We are happy and joyful at the birth of a child, on the occasion of marriage in the family, success in the examination or in some other venture, on getting a job or promotion in the job, upon acquisition of wealth and property and in many other similar cases of material gain, profit or success. It is natural to feel pleased in these situations which are pleasant but where is the need to show over-exuberance, gaiety, over-indulgence and unnecessary pomp and show? We all know how much time and money is actually wasted in these events of ostentation, out of false pride and ignorance. It is desirable to avoid all such unnecessary wastage.

Similarly, our moments of pain and misery may arise from physical discomfort, disease, material loss, failure, non-fulfilment of desires, abuse and dishonour, deficiency of some sort and last of all from death of a close friend or relative etc. Such happenings of real life may be viewed as exigencies of material life and these have to be accepted and endured with patience and determination. While one should make every effort to avoid painful situations for safety etc, yet the unavoidable happening of adversity has to he endured. It should always be borne in mind that for a normal individual there in no obligation to be overjoyed or overexcited in case of success or to feel utterly defected and miserable in case of failure.

To conclude, pleasure and pain both are bound to come and go in life. One must therefore face and go along the current flow of life. The key to face all situations is to endure. The struggle of life has to be sustained through dualities of life which include pleasure, pain, success, failure, joy, sorrow, honour, dishonour, health, disease, wealth and poverty, surfiet or deficiency and other ups and downs of material way of life. All these situations should be faced with courage, confidence, calmness and equal-mindedness.

Life shall then be at peace and prove purposeful.

Consequences of Material Path

According to the GITA, there are certain things in human life which are like NECTAR (or sweet) in the beginning and POISON (bitter) at the end. This holds good more or less in case of material path of life. We follow the material path of life in the hope of numerous enjoyments and happiness it offers. Food, dress, wealth, health, material possessions etc are some of the glaring examples. The ultimate aim of material life is to acquire happiness by enjoying so we are always in search of it by following the material path and our whole life becomes a wild-goose-chase for happiness, which most of the time eludes us. In short, in all our human efforts and activities, there is always an inner urge to be happy, in the background.

The question arises, do we get happiness in the material way of life. This question may be answered by saying that we do get sometimes, and don't at other times. If you ask a common man in the street 'Are you really happy in your life? He will come out with several problems and complaints. Perhaps nobody in this world, rich or poor, big or small is really happy in this world! That is why the great Guru Nanak uttered the saying '*Nanak dukhya sab sansar*.' The whole world is in pain or misery – in other words unhappy. Thus there is no real happiness in the material way of life.

Notwithstanding what has been stated above, we do find episodes of happiness here and there in our daily life. As we start our day and get up in the morning, some people who enjoyed sound sleep throughout night, without any terrifying dreams, they may look fresh and quite happy. But what about those who did not enjoy the pleasure of good night sleep? They would certainly look unhappy and lazy.

We try to find happiness through material means. Let us take some examples. Good tasty food and drinks make us feel happy as long as we consume these. What happens after some time when we again feel hungry and thirsty. Acquisition of wealth and material possession gives us happiness. But we are bound to feel unhappy when we lose these. We long to have children and feel happy at their birth, but feel dejected and most unhappy if they die or maltreat or desert us in old age. Marriage is one of the happiest occasions of material life. The same event brings grief and unhappiness when it ends in divorce or death of the spouse. All these examples and many more will lead us to the conclusion that material happiness is only temporary or short-lived. The great English novelist, Thomas Hardy had observed 'Happiness is only an episode in the general drama of pain in life'. Happiness, which is of transitory nature is not the desirable goal of human life.

It may also be observed that material happiness brings attachment and is of binding nature. If something gives us happiness, we become attached to it and would like to have more and more of it. Thus human beings develop an addiction for that thing, such as, tasty food, sweets, smoking, drinking, sexual gratification, etc. Their absence causes anger, dissatisfaction and unhappiness. Happiness of this nature leads us to bondage and its evil consequences.

We have already mentioned role of desires, pleasure and pain in material path of life, and their adverse effects on human life. All material desires bind us in unending cyclic order of pursuits for happiness, which is never to be found on permanent basis. The resulting insecurity and disappointment disturbs our peace of mind and thus leads us to unhappiness. The so called pleasures of life are mixed with pain or are followed by pain. These pleasures are also of temporary and binding nature.

On the basis of above discussion, it may be concluded that the material path looks rosy, tempting and has its mirth and merriment but it is not without pitfalls. In this context, it may be relevant to quote a verse from the UPANISHAD, as follows:-

> *"The face of TRUTH is covered with a GOLDEN VEIL. Uncover the reality, to the view of one devoted to truth."*
>
> [Ishopanishad .Verse.15.]

There is also a saying – All that glitters is not gold. The true reality hidden beneath the material path is somewhat different from its external appearance. The material path and its pleasures are like golden veil which hide the reality behind it. Most human beings get stuck in the glitter of the exterior golden face of the material path and thus remain out angled in its pleasures. Thus process of addiction to the pleasures of the material world is carried on from one birth to another in the vicious cycle of birth and death. Thus the material man is deprived of the ultimate truth and real goal of life which is eternal bliss and not the temporary glimpses of enjoyment which come and go and are also missed with pain.

Human life is a combination of matter and spirit. The material path as the name suggests is mainly embroiled into the material aspects of life. It by and large remains involved in the fulfilment of desires through sense gratification. Accordingly it gets entangled in the objects of the external world and neglects the inner – self which is the real master of human life. This path is therefore based on ignorance of reality, devoid of true knowledge and right understanding. It is, therefore full of desires tendencies and unsound practices.

This is the path which makes human life a mixed drama of pleasure and pain and other dualities of life which are binding. It may be pertinent to point out here that human life is not just by chance. It is not an imaginary play for fun and frolic or free for all aimless exercise. It is not in the least, one time chance to eat, drink and be merry! Life definitely is a serious venture. It is Gods gift to the individual soul to plan and embark upon the sacred journey of human life for progress and fulfilment leading to the final destination which in one word, may be described as PERFECTION in peace and happiness. This final stage or goal lies in the relation of the SUPREME SOUL and it culminates in eternal bliss or ANANDA.

WHAT is the way to attain that goal. Certainly it is not the material path. According to our holy scriptures the solution and the salvation from all pain and misery lies in practicing the SPIRITUAL PATH which we shall briefly discuss in the succeeding chapter.

The Spiritual Path

As the name suggests the spiritual path is mainly related to the spirit, which is the life force behind the functioning of the material body.

Human life is a unique combination of material body and the spirit (SOUL). The material body works in conjunction with the soul and it acts as the instrument or vehicle of the soul. In the spiritual path, body, mind and soul have to be kept pure, healthy and in good cheer. This is done through the effective and righteous use of the material means combined with the spiritual means. The spiritual path is based upon true knowledge, righteousness and real wisdom. The pure soul has to assume full control over the body, senses and the mind. The practice of this path builds a bridge between the lower spirit (individual soul) and the Higher Spirit (Supreme Soul) and this establishes an intimate close contact between the two. An individual has to make all –out efforts to know the reality of God, nature (prakriti) and the soul. A genuine follower of the spiritual path does not crave for or run after material pursuits which involve fulfilment of mundane desires. He tries to look beyond the manifest world and its temporary pleasures, in order to discover the reality of life and its final goal.

The spiritual path does not necessarily mean following of formal religious rituals of a conventional religion. On the other hand, it involves inculcation of a genuine holy attitude and way of life based on the practice of righteous actions in daily life. The emphasis is on the miner discipline rather than external modes of ritual worship. Thus a person can be spiritual without going to a religious place of worship, like temple, mosque, church, gurudwara etc. It also does not mean renunciation of household and domestic life and duties. One has to perform ones duties and fulfil essential responsibilities of one's daily life. However while doing so he has to exercise self-restraint and keep his mind and senses under full control practice discrimination between right and wrong and perform all actions in a spirit of detachment. He must keep God in mind while performing various actions in all walks of life. The practice of spiritual path includes practice of moral values in thought, word and deed, study of good literature, good company, charity and service to the needy and deserving persons, honest and straight dealings in public life, prayer and meditation, practice of truth, love and non-violence in the real sense. One is required to live a simple life, maintain good health and moral conduct and practice righteousness in all possible manners. It does not necessarily mean leaving home, going to forest, living in an ashram and dress in a particular fashion. Thus one can practice spiritual path while even living in the material world performing all assigned duties and desirable actions of daily life in the right way.

Primarily, God is the main focus of spiritual path. It is the feeling or experience of intimacy which one shares with God; it is the bond which an individual soul establishes with the supreme soul. It is the practice of deepest faith and devotion for HIM. It involves complete self-surrender to the Divine Will. It is the awareness of the knowledge of the true reality and the implementation of this knowledge in real life. It is the practice of moral conduct and discipline that leads to God and eternal bliss. Spirituality, therefore involves remembering God and feeling this presence at all times as far as possible. It does not merely mean that one has to sit silent with eyes closed and doing no work. What it really means is having an inbuilt feeling of God's presence while doing anything or even inaction. One should feel God's influence within one self and repose full trust in Him every moment of one's life. It is trying to establish close contact with God. Thus, spirituality is the ever-flowing activity of the mind that discovers the reality of all- pervading existence, that brings fulfilment and freedom from worldly bondage.

In contrast with the material path where an individual mostly thinks of himself and members of his family, spirituality involves loving all creation and believing in the welfare of all. Practice of ethical values, in all walks of life is a by-product of spirituality. A spiritual life is devoid of all vices which include anger, hatred, lust, greed, false pride, ignoble desires, deception, dishonesty, injustice, malice etc. The practice of spirituality involves inner detachment and disconnection with material desires and acquisitions. As a practitioner advances on the spiritual path, he realizes that he requires only very few material objects for his body, household and daily needs. His desires and personal requirements become very limited and are restricted to the barest minimum. Thus he requires less food less clothing and the least money and material possessions. There is also gradual disconnection at the level of KARMA. A spiritual person has no desire to do something or the other merely to fulfill some material desire. As a matter of fact, he has no mundane desires except the minimum essential to maintain his body. He performs his minimal functions and keeps always from unnecessary acts and cravings.

The practice of the spiritual path needs the assistance of the body, the mind and the intellect. It is with the help of the body, and the intellect that the mind has to be purged of all undesirable and evil tendencies and thus keep the individual spirit pure and undefiled. The closeness between the individual soul which works within the body and the supreme soul is possible only when the body and the mind are purged of all vices. In the epic MAHABHARATA, there is mention of 13 specific evils which include lust, anger, greed, attachment, ego, worry, fear, anxiety, indecision, impatience, grief, dependence and jealousy etc. The first five (5) are considered the most dangerous. The GITA describes the first three, lust, anger, and greed as three gates to hell. The above mentioned negative tendencies which are deemed as SINS defile the mind and cover the soul with the veil of ignorance. These retard the progress on the spiritual path.

Progress in the spiritual path, brings more control at the level of body, speech and mind. One is able to control one's feelings, emotions, and wild expressions. A person who has advanced on the spiritual path has the least likes and dislikes. He has no spare time for idle gossip and unproductive discussion etc. He devotes his time in the practice of silence and solitude, in meditation, prayer and concentration on God, study of spiritual literature and in the unselfish service of living beings. He maintains love for all and hatred for none. Progress in spirituality comes gradually and after continuous long practice. Firm faith in God, true devotion and persistent detachment are essential tools to attain higher levels of spirituality which means higher consciousness. Spiritual wisdom downs after the actual experience of higher consciousness. The spiritual path is difficult and the progress is slow with ups and downs in between. Constant remembrance of God, regular study of scriptures with right understanding, practice of moral conduct in daily life, practice of yogic discipline (SADHNA) for a long time are some of the essential requirements for attaining success in the spiritual path.

Mere performance of religions rituals, parrot-like recitation of Gods name or reading from scriptures without right understanding and without practice of moral conduct in real life, is far from the practice of spiritual path.

Spirituality is the gift of God to a noble soul. It builds a bridge of love and friendship between the individual soul and the supreme soul. The practice of spiritual path provides inner strength and leads to the equanimity of mind and mental peace. It strengthens determination and self-confidence to face successfully all challenges of worldly life. The successful pursuit of spiritual path ultimately leads to God realisation, wherein lives eternal happiness (ANANDA) which is the real goal of human life. In view of the extremely difficult discipline (TAPASYA) required to be followed in the pursuit of the spiritual path, only a few rare individuals dare to practice this path.

A devotee who has achieved sufficient progress in the spiritual path displays some signs which are briefly mentioned as follows:-

i) At the physical level there is disconnection with material objects. There is less need for food, clothing etc. There is also less urge for action. One would like to perform only essential actions as a matter of ones duty.

ii) At the level of mind, there is disconnection with pleasure and pain and other dualities of life. One gets contented with what one gets and there are no complaints. There are also no likes and dislikes.

iii) The ultimate sign which comes at the highest level is that of VAIRAGYA. It is the stage of total absence of attachment for any material object. In this stage the entire universe becomes his home and he attains the highest devotion to God and love for all creation without any discrimination of any kind. He becomes devoid of all evil and remains engrossed in the worship of God till his soul leaves the body and joins the supreme soul.

Means to Spiritual Path

Worship of God

There are different ways to practice the spiritual path based on religious beliefs, traditions and social environment, etc but the final goal remains the same – God–realization. As God is the chief focus of spiritual path, worship of ONE God alone is the highest means to practice spiritual path. The worship of God based on VEDIC principles has the following three parts which are briefly mentioned below:-

I) Glorification of God (Stuti) – God is invisible and formless. As such He can be understood mainly by his attributes which are numerous. Therefore the first step is to remember God on the basis of his positive main attributes in the following manner:-

'The SUPREME pervades every where. He is all powerful, all energy, pure, perfect, eternal and self-existent. RULER of all has eternal knowledge and all bliss. He is never born, never commits sin and is free from pain, grief and ignorance and the like. These are only examples and more may be added if the devotes so desires.

The OBJECT of glorification of God is to keep his attributes in view and mould ones life and conduct on the basis of these attributes, as far as possible after their proper understanding with full faith and understanding. Just parrot-like repetition of different names of God is neither desirable nor beneficial. The object is to reform ones character and conduct, considering the attributes and character of God as the IDEAL.

II) Prayer To God (Prarthana) – Prayer is the means to seek God's help and inspiration for desirable ends. One should pray to God for true knowledge, purity and strength of mind, courage to face all odds and wisdom to remove all ignorance and so on, it does not mean that one has to do nothing and everything has to be left to God. First of all one has to make all efforts to attain the object of one's prayer and only then one becomes qualified to his grace and help. There is a popular saying. God helps those who help themselves. This has to be followed before seeking God's help. Prayer instils confidence.

Prayer is opening of one's heart to the supreme and not a mere ritual. It is pure conversation with HIM. It is an individuals' effort to come close to God and to feel HIS presence. It is an act of purification of mind and soul. Prayer lifts individual consciousness to a higher level and is a conscious attempt to establish a meaningful relation with God.

A prayer which is said without any selfish motive is the best.

III) Communion (Upasana.) –The word 'upasana' really means–to come close to. In this context, the Upanishad says as follows:-

No tongue can express that bliss which flows from communion with the supreme, into the soul of that man whose impurities are washed away, by the practice of yoga, whose mind being turned away from the external world gets centered in the supreme spirit, because that bliss is felt by the soul in its inner self alone.

In order to come close to the SUPREME SPIRIT, one has to first qualify for it. What is required is the purity of mind that should be free from any attachment and malice. All senses have to be under full control of the mind.

The intellect should function properly and in the right direction. The sense of individuality (ego) should cease to function. The individual soul has to merge in the supreme soul.

Swami Dayananda Saraswati, the founder of Arya Samaj in his book '*Satyarath Prakash*' has briefly indicated the method of doing worship, as follows:-

When a man desires to engage in upasna, let him resort to a solitary clean place and get comfortably seated, practice pranayam (control of breath), restrain the senses from the pursuit of external objects and fix the mind on one of the following places: the naval, the heart, the throat, the middle of the eyes, the top of the head or the spine. Let him then discriminate between his own soul and the supreme soul and get absorbed in the contemplation of the latter and thus commune with HIM. One should contemplate in this way, at least, one hour daily. The more one involves in such practice, the greater one can advance spiritually. By practice, one will know gradually, as to on which point, one should fix the mind and feel at case and be in peace. Regular daily practice will produce good results.

The GITA also mentions some practical hints for the technique of meditation, as in the following verses:-

> *'Shutting out all external objects, fixing the vision between the eyebrows, making even the inward and the outward breaths moving within*

the nostrils, the sage who has controlled the senses, mind and understanding, who is intent on liberation, who has cast away desire, fear and anger, he is ever freed.'

(Verses 27- 28 – Chapter V)

These verses briefly describe the method of meditation along with some conditions which are required to be fulfilled. Liberation is the goal of meditation. This method of meditation is further supplemented in another verse as follows:-

Let the yogi try constantly to concentrate his mind on the SUPREME, remaining in solitude alone, self- controlled free from desire and greed.

Verse10 – Chapter-IV

In CHAPTER VI of the GITA, there are several verses which indicate how meditation should be actually practiced through physical and mental discipline. This chapter lays down some specific conditions or requirements for achieving progress in this path. These are briefly summarized below:-

1. The aspirant must be free from desires and longings for possessions.

2. One must practice moderation in eating, sleeping and re-creative activities.

3. Firm faith in God is utmost essential.

4. Practice restraint in all walks of life.

5. Fixed place and time for meditation is more useful.

6. One should sit in the right posture in which one can sit undisturbed for a long lime.

The process of meditation requires complete self control. The mind should be kept free from selfish and unnecessary desires. This is a difficult discipline which needs long constant practice and a proper mental attitude. The supreme happiness can be achieved only when the mind becomes peaceful, pure and devoid of passions.

Yoga Practice

Yoga is the most effective means to practice the spiritual path. The GITA which expounds the philosophy of yoga in a comprehensive manner describes three main forms of yoga. The following verse in the GITA indicates the close connection between worship and yoga:-

[Those who fixing their mind on Me worship Me, ever earnest and possessed of supreme faith–them do I consider most perfect in yoga.]

[Verse 2 - Chapter XII]

The Gita is full of numerous references to yoga. However there are three main paths which are briefly described below.

Karma Yoga (Path Of Action)

Life is full of action and no one can remain without doing work. All human beings are bound by the results of their actions. According to this law of nature, every action has its reaction and thus is a source of bondage. The Gita tells us the way to perform action, as stated in the following verse:-

[Fixed in yoga, do thy work, abandoning attachment with an even mind in success or failure, for evenness of mind is called yoga.']

[Verse 48. Chapter.II]

All work in life, should be performed with equal – mindedness without attachment. Success and failure should not result in emotional ups and downs.

The essential principle and the essence of the philosophy of karma yoga is contained in the most famous following verse:-

[To action, you have a right and never at all to its fruits, but not the fruits of action be thy motive, neither let there be in thou any attachment to in-action.]

[Verse 47.chapter.II]

In real life, when we do something, the act of doing is within our reach but its result is beyond our control as besides our efforts there are other extraneous factors also which influence the outcome of our action. Thus the fruits of our actions may or may not be according to our expectations. However it does not imply that we should not perform action or make no efforts on the plea that results are beyond us.

The Gita also lays stress on understanding (intelligence) while performing action. Thus action should be performed with understanding but without concern for its fruits, free from like and dislike and with the thought of God within. Thus there is atmost emphasis on the close kinship with the SUPREME while performing all actions. Keeping God in mind always, one is expected to perform only desirable pure actions. Of all the different paths described in the Gita, KARMA Yoga seems more suited to the householder as every householder has to perform actions in the form of obligatory duties. Karma yoga which in brief is the path of right actions without attachment to its fruits, has greater role to play in the lives of vast majority of people. In this context the main teachings of the Gita are summarised below:-

1. All actions should be performed with proper understanding and even-mindedness.
2. Action as a matter of duty should be performed in a spirit of sacrifice to the SUPREME and without any sense of egotism.
3. All normal activities should be carried on without being obsessed by desire and a bsorbed in the thought of God. Such an attitude will guide a person towards the path of righteousness.
4. Action and knowledge should go together. It is said that action without knowledge is blind and knowledge without action is lame.

5. Action should be performed without concern for its fruits. Always feel pleasure in doing your duty without worrying about the impending result. Work should be done for its own rake.
6. One should understand ones physical and mental capabilities which determine our nature and act accordingly.

The above discussion briefly describes the path of action or Karma Yoga. In the spiritual path of life all actions are required to be performed in the light of instructions laid down in Karma Yoga. The purity of spirit achieved by performing all actions in this manner will invite the grace of God which will help the devotee to attain the highest goal of life.

The Gita mentions about two–fold way of life as indicated in the following verse:-

> *'In this world a two–fold way of life has been taught by me, the path of knowledge for men of contemplation and that of works for men of action.'*
>
> [Verse 3- Chapter III]

As indicated above, human beings may be broadly classified into following two types:-

i) Those whose mental disposition is towards ACTION or worldly pursuit.

ii) Those who have the tendency to explore the inner- self.

For obvious reasons the path of Action or Karma Yoga will be more suitable for the first type of persons while the path of knowledge or Gyan yoga will be more practicable for the second type.

Both these paths are equally efficient means for the spiritual way of life but these are intended for two different types of individuals because of their different mental dispositions. We have already described the Karma Yoga, and shall now briefly discuss the Gyan Yoga or path of knowledge.

Gyan Yoga (Path Of Knowledge)

Gyan yoga is suitable for those who are more inclined towards contemplation of inner-self. Gyan Yoga or path of knowledge as the name suggests is the path of enlightenment as opposed to ignorance which giv es rise to material desires and thus leads to bondage. So long as ignorance persists, the final goal of liberation can not be achieved. True knowledge is the means to remove ignorance. It is the light which illumines the soul and gives divine experience. In order to achieve this, the soul has to be cleansed of all accompanying impurities of human blemishes, such as, anger, lust, false pride, greed, fear and attachment, besides all selfish desires.

The Gita provides the fundamentals of this knowledge. It gives the knowledge of the supreme the individual self and material nature. It explains the differences between the individual self and the body in which it resides. It indicates the causes of pleasure and pain, misery and human body etc. It tells us how we can have even mind by uniting our intellect with the Divine and by renouncing the fruits of all our actions. It also tells us how to perform actions and to remain calm in all circumstances and situations of human life. It also tells us about the immortality of the spirit and helps in the proper understanding of existence. It shows the way that leads to stable intelligence through contentment and by patting away all the desires of the mind.

Gyan yoga is the product of mind and intellect of an individual, while his thoughts rest in God. In this yoga, the right understanding becomes the main instrument of spiritual realization by lifting the individual consciousness to the supreme consciousness. The way of true knowledge lies through the lanes of unflinching faith, constant devotion and worship. The following verses from the Gita show the way:-

> *"To those who are constantly devoted and worship ME with love, I grant the concentration of understanding by which they come unto Me".*
>
> [Verse 10. Chapter. X]

> *"Out of compassion for these same ones, remaining within My own state, I destroy the darkness of ignorance by the shining lamp of wisdom."*
>
> [Verse 11. Chapter. X]

The Gita not only tells the theory of knowledge but also gives the practical tips on how to acquire that knowledge. The way to divine knowledge requires constant devotion and worship of God. If these requirements are met, true knowledge will descend upon a devotee by god's grace. Out of compassion for such determined devotees who worship God with love and adoration, God removes the veil of their ignorance and grants them spiritual wisdom by which they reach him. However, this will not happen all of a sudden. One has to traverse the spiritual path for a long distance and time with steady understanding and reach the final phase through the constant practice of mental control and self-discipline. The fires of passion, selfish desires and attachment must be extinguished. One has to control the senses and the revolving mind but this is not to be achieved through suppression but through regular steady practice with the thought of God in mind always and thus drawing inspiration and confidence from his ever-existing presence. This should be done with a spirit of willing sacrifice and self-surrender to the will of God. Every form of self-control where one willingly and lovingly sacrifices enjoyment of senses, is a means to attain true knowledge.

True knowledge can also be gained through regular process of learning, as declared in the following verse of the Gita:-

> *'LEARN that by humble reverence, by enquiry and by service. The men of wisdom who have seen the TRUTH will instruct thee in knowledge.'*

[Verse 34- Chapter IV]

Man can always be a learner. The whole life-time offers a vast opportunity for learning through everyday experiences. The spiritual knowledge can be attained from competent guides and genuine gurus who themselves have already attained true knowledge and have become full of wisdom. But these are some conditions attached to learning from such holy guides and men of wisdom. The disciple has to show them full reverence in all humility, by asking them questions for removing any doubts and by serving them with love and sincerity. The ancient tradition of leasing at the holy feet of a rishi (spiritual master) in his ashram is a befitting example of learning process and gaining true knowledge. In the process of learning mere theoretical learning from a book, etc is not sufficient to acquire true knowledge. The acquisition essentially includes a deep insight into the knowledge of TRUTH and constancy in the knowledge of the spirit besides, practice of moral values in real life.

A common question may arise – what is the effect or role of true knowledge in the spiritual path? A clean and concise answer to this question is that all ignorance is removed when true knowledge is gained. All doubts get cleared and what was earlier obscure becomes visible. A person who has attained knowledge has complete control over his senses and his desires and his mind attains peace and rests in God. It may be concluded that there is nothing on earth equal in purity to true knowledge which is equated with pure wisdom (as against material knowledge and worldly wisdom), as stated in the following verse of the Gita:-

"[There is nothing on earth, equal in purity to wisdom. He who becomes perfected by yoga finds this of himself, in his self, in course of time.]"

[Verse 38-Chapter-IV]

The above discussion shows how Gyan Yoga can play an effective role in the spiritual path of life. We shall now briefly deal with BHAKTI YOGA or the path of Devotion.

Bhakti Yoga (Path Of Devotion)

BHAKTI Yoga which means Devotion to God is another effective means to follow the spiritual path. Devotion is the path of intense love for God. It is not merely physical attention or a religions ritual nor intellectual appreciation. It is love not for things material but love for the highest ideal which means it is love at the level of the SUPREME. It is not superficial, not external adoration but it emanates from the depth of the inner -self. Devotion to God is the highest and the purest form of love. Love in the ordinary sense may be fascination or physical attraction for a person or an object etc. Such love is limited, changeable and temporary. We may call it attachment.

Bhakti or Devotion is spontaneous, from the very heart and for a higher cause or object. Simply going to a temple or any place of worship or performing some specific religious rituals on certain occasions is not necessarily devotion. Devotion involves intense love and longing without any sensual enjoyment.

In Bhakti Yoga the devotee has to acquire and practice certain qualities which enable him to follow this discipline of the spiritual path. There is great emphasis on such divine qualities rather than mere performance of some religious rituals. Broadly speaking, these qualities are moral values which include love, humility, mercy, gentleness, ever- mindedness, contentment, self-restraint, firm determination, absence of egoism, anger and fear, besides greed and attachment and some more of similar nature. The service of humanity, without any ulterior motives is an essential aspect of devotion.

There are several verses in the Gita which clearly indicate the qualities of a true devotee, as follows:-

'He who has no ill will to any being, who is friendly and compassionate, free from egoism and self-sense, even- minded in pleasure and pain and patient.'

[Verse 13 – Chapter - XII]

'He who does work for Me, he who looks upon Me as his goal, he who worships Me, free from attachment, he who is free from enmity to all creatures, he goes to Me'.

[Verse 55 – Chapter - XI]

'Those who fixing their minds on me worship me, ever earnest and possessed of supreme faith, them do I consider most perfect in yoga'.

[Verse 2 - Chapter - XII]

Bhakti yoga or the path of devotion can lead to perfection and achieve the highest goal of life. Devotion does not exclude action but has to be performed without attachment and as a sacrifice to God. Devotion thus includes action without attachment, friendliness to all, compassion freedom from enmity and egoism, besides full understanding which dwells on the supreme. It implies worship of God with complete faith.

Constant remembrances of God with full faith, contemplation of his attributes, singing his praises, performing actions without attachment, in the spirit of reverence and service to God, and practice of qualities mentioned earlier in real conduct of life, form part of discipline of devotion or bhakti yoga. Faith is the cornerstone of devotion. The Gita tells us that those who worship God with supreme faith and earnestness are the most perfect in yoga. This view is expressed in the following verse :-

'Those who fixing their mind on Me worship Me ever earnest and endowed with supreme faith, them I consider most perfect in yoga.'

Earnestness and unswerving faith in God are the main ingredients of the act of devotion. The true devotee meditates on God with true love and all his actions are God-oriented. All his thoughts are fixed on HIM. Devotion involves complete surrender to the supreme. The path of devotion rests its stand upon love and emotions of a person and directs these towards God. Individual ego is destroyed by the intensity of love for God. It does not take into account the reflection and the reasoning of the mind and makes full use of love and adoration of the Divine. It consists of the yearning of the eager heart and seeks divine fulfilment of the emotional aspects of a person.

Devotion is the direct straight and sure means to reach God, by following the spiritual path of life. In this context, attention of the readers is invited towards the following famous verse of the Gita:-

'By unswerving devotion to Me O' ARJUNA, I can be thus known, truly seen and entered into'.

[Verse 54- Chapter-XI]

The experience of God can be achieved through unswerving devotion of God.

The role of devotion in the spiritual path of life is of utmost importance. This is the sure means to reach God. To conclude, the attention of the readers may be drawn towards the following two verses of the Gita :-

'On Me fix thy mind, to Me be devoted, worship Me, rever Me, thus having disciplined thyself, with Me as the goal, to Me shalt thou come.'

[Verse 34- Chapter IX]

'Fix thy mind on Me, be devoted to Me, sacrifice to Me prostrate thyself before me, so shalt thou come to Me. I promise thee truly, for thou art dear to me.'

[Verse 65- Chapter-XVIII]

The three paths of yoga discipline may look separate but these are inter-linked and are not separate water-tight compartments. These are mentioned separately to suit persons of different temperaments. It does not mean that a single particular path has to be followed rigidly by a certain individual. The practice of a particular path by an individual depends, by and large, upon the nature of the practitioner. In actual practice these paths can not be practiced is isolation, but in proper combination as these are inter-twined to achieve the final goal of life.

To start with one has to practice a particular path, influenced by his innate attitude. For instance, an action-oriented person should follow the path of action or karma yoga. But while doing so, he needs knowledge in order to discriminate between right and wrong, good or bad action. Besides he also has to practice devotion to God in some form of worship or service to God or humanity. Similarly a man with a temperament for devotion or having propensity for knowledge and contemplation has also to perform some action as no one in this world can remain without action. The purity of mind acquired by the constant practice of righteous actions and by the acquisition and assimilation of right knowledge would lead to devotion. Similarly a person of firm devotion acquires purity of thought and right knowledge and therefore he would perform right actions. Thus right knowledge, right action and true devotion cannot be separated and all these three paths have to he fused together in the spiritual path of life. Thus the triple path of yoga works together to form a single system of self-offering to the supreme. In this way a synthesis of various strands of spirituality paves the way for the harmonious development of human personality towards perfection. Action, Knowledge and Devotion are blended together for the divine fulfilment of man. The spiritual path of life makes use of all these three ingredients. The correct understanding of the fundamental creation (i.e. God, nature and soul) performance of right actions, without concern for surrender to God – all these ingredients work in harmony to achieve God-realization which is the ultimate and true goal of human life.

Ashtang Yoga

Eight Fold Path of Yoga

ASHTANG YOGA which means yoga of eight parts was founded by Mahrishi Patanjali. It is the complete system of yoga discipline and as such is a very effective means to follow the spiritual path which leads to God- realization. Its eight parts are very briefly, mentioned below:-

I & II **Yamas and Niyamas**. There are ten principles which are required to be observed in the conduct of daily life. Five yamas are as follows:-

Ahimsa (non-violence), Satya [Truth], Non-stealing (Asteya), Brahmacharya (Celibacy and self-control) Aparigraha (Non- greed or non-accumulation of material objects).

The yamas are broad-based social and universal virtues which are in the form of moral restraints or social obligations. The practice of these virtues is indispensable to follow the spiritual path.

Niyamas are also five, as follows:-

i) **SHAUCHA** (Cleanliness–external and internal) SANTOSHA (contentment) TAPA (austerity) SWADHYAY (study of scriptures) and Ishwar Pranidhan (surrender to God).

ii) **Niyamas** are the means of personal discipline which is extremely essential to follow the spiritual path. The YAMAS and NIYAMAS, both combined constitute the personal and social code of conduct.

iii) **Asana** This is the third part of ashtang yoga. It is essential to practice meditation in the spiritual path. For this purpose a stable and comfortable sitting posture of the body is called asana. One can practice meditation for a long time in this posture.

iv) **Pranayam** (Regulation of breath) This is the fourth part of Ashtang Yoga. It helps in purifying and controlling the mind.

v) **Pratyahara**. This is the process by which the mind and the senses are withdrawn from the external world and are directed inwards.

vi to viii) **DHARMA DAYANA AND SAMADHI** – These are all parts of an internal difficult discipline which involves focusing, contemplation and concentration of mind.

Note: The author has within a book 'The essence of Mahrishi Patanjali's' Ashtang Yoga which contains description of all eight parts in some detail. The book has been published by **Pustak Mahal, Darya Ganj, New Delhi.** Readers may like to consult the book for more details on Ashtang Yoga.

Material Path v/s Spiritual Path -A Comparison

We have already examined in some detail the two paths, material and spiritual to live life. Let us now draw a brief comparison of these two paths sand make up our mind to which path we should follow.

Every one in this world wants happiness in life. In modern times, happiness through material means is the most sought-after commodity. Most people want to grow rich, have material possessions and enjoy life through delicious food, fun and good fortune. There is ever increasing craze for worldly pleasures and pleasantries by following the material paths, and thus acquiring the maximum possible happiness through fair or foul means. Nobody bothers to care about the means and also consider as to how long that happiness lasts. There is no denying the fact that wealth and material means can provide comfort and make a person happy. At the same time, it is also a fact that such happiness is temporary and lasts as long as we indulge in it. For instance, delicious food and sweets make us feel happy as we enjoy consuming these. After some time we feel hungry again and our enjoyment fades away. In case of delicious food, one is also likely to overeat because of its good taste which overpowers our discretion. The result of overeating may cause pain in the stomach and if over-indulgence becomes a habit it may lead to serious adverse consequences in the form of some chronic disease or disorder. A wealthy person is always afraid of losing his wealth. Every day several cases of theft, robbery, deceit and death are reported in the press. Excessive wealth leads to its misuse and wastage in various evil and unsocial practices. It is said in the bible that money is the root of all evils. Take another case of sexual indulgence which is the most popular means of enjoyment and human happiness. Excess of sexual indulgence leads to loss of good health and some sex- related incurable diseases of which HIV has become most common these days. Similarly various other means of material path can lead to undesirable consequences. In short the following adverse consequences are always linked with the practice of material path:-

1. The happiness gained through material path is temporary. No one is really happy in his whole life or even for a greater part of life.

2. Such happiness is either mixed with pain or is followed by pain. Pleasure and pain take their turns in the material path of life.

3. Material path does not lead to the ultimate goal of life which is God–realisation or freedom from pain and misery and eternal happiness (ANANDA).

Let us now examine the case of spiritual path. The situation in case of SPIRITUAL PATH is entirely different. Here the happiness is linked with the source. God is the source of ETERNAL BLISS, free from any pain or misery. According to VEDAS, God is the friend (MITRA) and well-wisher of all. Spiritual path is the way that leads to God, the source and individual souls can also attain eternal bliss from that source. The advancement in spiritual path pulls out a practitioner from the quicksand of material mess and disconnects him from the worldly attachments and their evil effects.

All worldly people who are engrossed in worldly pleasures derived from wealth, name and fame and other similar material means get intoxicated and their mind and conscience are entangled in a vicious circle of sensual enjoyments. Just as a drunkard cannot take case of himself, in the same way such intoxicated persons become enslaved to material bondage. The excessive enjoyment of sensual pleasures render him helpless and he is unable to save himself from their adverse effects. The final result of such enslavement and addiction to material pleasures is utter ruin. It is only when he comes out of stage of intoxication that he can regain proper consciousness and move in the right direction. This is possible only by following the spiritual path which teaches the practice of righteousness, true worship and acquisition of right knowledge.

A proper understanding of the two paths, material and spiritual and their comparison should enable a person to make the right choice. There is no bar on the proper and right enjoyment of material means of happiness but it has to be kept within reasonable and beneficial limits. In fact, it is necessary for an individual to enjoy all good and useful things to live life but one should always keep in mind that the happiness resulting from material path are temporary and illusory. Constant contemplation of this thought must prevail upon him to direct all his efforts towards the attainment of spiritual happiness which is lasting and free from any type of pain and misery. The final goal of life is eternal bliss, after gaining which nothing more remains to he gained. One must therefore direct all efforts to attain this goal which is possible only by following the SPIRITUAL PATH. It is for you to make a choice!

Material v/s Spiritual

Interesting Anecdotes

King Akbar and the Hermit

During the reign of King Akbar, a hermit lived in a nearby forest and many people came to him to seek advice and help. The hermit wanted to entertain and help them but he was always short of money. So he went to Akbar for help. When he entered the palace, he found the king in prayer and overheard the king asking God to give him more wealth and power. Hearing this the hermit turned back. The king saw him and asked the reason for coming and leaving soon without saying anything.

The holy man said "I come to you to get some money for entertaining my visitors. But here I found that you too are begging from God. So I thought: *What can I get from a beggar*! I will now beg from God. Saying this the hermit went away.

Moral. In the material life, even a king is not content with his wealth. God is the real giver of all things. The spiritual path leads to God.

Alexander the Great and the Yogi

Before his invasion of India, Akbar had heard stories of spiritual saints and yogis of India. After winning battles when he was about to return to his country, he was advised to pay visit to a popular yogi, who lived and meditated in a forest, all alone.

Alexander went to the yogi and asked him to accompany the former, promising him great wealth, high honour and various comforts.

The yoga refused his offer and said 'I do not need your wealth and comforts. I am very happy here.' Alexander was astonished and impressed and went away to his country.

Moral. A person truly devoted to God does not need any thing from anybody. He can ignore all temptations offered even by a great king like Alexander.

Empty Hands of Alexander

Alexander, a great warrior conquered several kingdoms and became a great emperor. He looted a lot of valuables and amassed a huge treasure. But he died at a young age after suffering from a terrible illness in spite of his best efforts and treatment.

Just before his death, he realized that all his accumulated wealth was of no use to him and he has to leave everything behind, consequent upon his death!

Upon his death, and according to his previous instructions, when his coffin was being carried, while his body was covered, his both hands were spread out naked and empty. This was to show that he come empty-handed at his birth and went empty-handed at his death! All material possessions are left behind after death.

Moral. There is no use of being greedy and amassing huge wealth. Contentment is the greatest wealth.

The Secret of Peace

Lord Buddha was sitting in the company of his disciples and a prince was also sitting nearby. The faces of disciples reflected spiritual peace and cheerfulness while the prince looked sad and gloomy.

A wise visitor to the Lord noted the difference and asked Buddha 'Sir in spite of their hard life your disciples are full of peace and delight, while the prince who has all the facilities and comforts, looks sad and without cheer. Please enlighten me why is this so?

Buddha smiled and said 'This is so because my disciples maintain evenness of mind and their mental peace is not disturbed by any happening. They do not brood over the past and worry about the future. This is the secret of their peace and cheerfulness.

Moral. Evenness of mind leads to peace in all situations. This is yoga.

I am the King

As LORD MAHAVIRA was passing over a sandy path, he left his footprints. An astrologer saw these and guessed them to be the foot marks of a great king. He followed these marks and soon found Mahavira standing.

He enquired whether he was a king, to which Mahavira replied, 'Yes I am the king.'

The astrologer asked, 'Then where is your army?

Lord said, 'I do not need an army as I have no enemy. The man asked 'What about your kingdom?'

Mahavira said, 'My body is my kingdom. I am king of myself.

Moral. Mahavira had attained the state of spiritual perfection, after which there is no need of any material objects kingdom or army.

How to Live Life

Rama Krishna Paramhansa delivered the following sermon to his disciples:-

Live in the world like a maid servant in a rich man's house. She performs all her household duties and also brings up the masters child whom she addresses as my son. However she knows quite well that neither the house where she works and lives and nor the child whom she calls my son belong to her. While she does her job, her mind dwells on her native place. Likewise, do your worldly duties, but fix your mind on God. Know that the house where you live, the family to which you belong do not really belong to you, they are all God's. You are simply his servant.

Moral. Always remember God and know the reality of life.

The Way to Peace

A sadhu said to Swami Vivekananda 'Swami Ji, I have relinquished everything to attain peace but I have not got it. I am perplexed, pleased guide me.'

Swami Ji said 'I will tell you the way to peace but you will have to do as I say.'

The sadhu said 'Yes, I will do, please tell me.'

Swami Ji said 'Leave your hut. If you find anyone hungry, feed him. If you meet anyone thirsty, give him water. If you find a sick needy person, get him medicine. Give clothing to the poor and help the needy in whatever way you can. By acting in this way, you will attain peace.'

Moral. By doing service to the needy or the poor, you can get peace. Feel joy in giving to the deserving.

The Most Surprising

This is an anecdote from Mahabharata, the great epic. Yamaraja, the Lord of death, asked Yudhishtra. What is the most surprising thing in the world.'

Yudhishtra replied 'The most surprising thing is that a person sees his friend, relatives and other persons dying, but he still behaves, as if death shall never touch him! Death is an inevitable phenomenon, yet most people carry on with their lives, unmindful of this stark reality.

Moral. We should realise the significance of both life and death and live life in the knowledge of wisdom of this reality.

Learn Detachment

Ramakrishna, the great saint used to advise his followers to practice detachment.

To press his point, he would cite the example of a dry coconut. It is difficult to shell out copra from a green coconut, as it remains attached to the inner walls of the coconut. But in a dry coconut, it is easy to get out, even without breaking it, as it has detached itself from the hard dry shell. Such is the advantage of detachment. Therefore learn detachment in your daily life, in thought, word and deed.

Moral: Detachment brings freedom from fear worry and even pain.

Tyagi (One Who Sacrifices)

A greedy rich fat man was indulging in many evil practices. Inspite of his wealth, he was unhappy. So he went to a renowned saint. He was much impressed by the saints' discourse and simple honest living. In admiration, he told the saint that he was a great Tyagi. The saint said 'But you are a greater Tyagi'. When the rich man asked how, the saint said "I have sacrificed this material world, but you have scarificed even god. Who is the creator of this world!"

The rich man realised his folly, felt ashamed and transformed himself into a pious man and a servant of God by following the spiritual way of life. Thereafter, he lived a happy, simple, contented life.

Moral: Perform good deeds and surrender to God to attain true happiness.

The Middle Path

After reading what has been written before, a discerning reader must have become familiar with the pros and cons of the two paths to live life. To recapitulate, the material path is more attractive and popular because of its immediate and visible benefits but it does not lead to perfection and total happiness. The spiritual path is the most desirable but is very difficult to pursue because of its restraints, restrictions and rectitude, but it leads to the attainment of the final goal of life. In view of the divergent differences in two paths, a common man would find himself in a dilemma – what to do, which way to go? For such persons who can not follow or do not wish to follow either of these two paths singly or exclusively, there is the choice of the Middle path. In this path one has to keep a balance between the practices of both the paths. This it is a mixture of both the material and spiritual paths.

Since the material path leads us to nowhere but to an unending vicious cycle of birth and death and the spiritual path is extremely difficult to pursue to its culmination, most human beings should follow the middle path which combines some share from the both. Obviously, one has to live life in the material world, perform actions, fulfil desires and so on.

There is therefore no escape from the material path for an average person. Therefore, the desirable course to follow should be to perform good actions and keep desires within proper limits. It should also be kept in mind that good actions lead to good results and bad actions would result in pain and misery. If we are unable to follow the spiritual path fully because of hardships involved in its pursuit we can at least, perform desirable good actions and thus avoid at least some of the adverse effects of material path by limiting our desires of greed, sensual indulgence etc by leading an honest simple life.

While enjoying the pleasures of material path within proper limits and by exercising appropriate control over the senses, one can enlighten the inner-self to some extent. Even while following the material path, there should be no difficulty in remembering God, conducting simple prayer and meditation for seeking God's blessings and guidance for leading a righteous life. There is nothing wrong in earning lots of money and in attaining professional success and in acquiring worldly possessions but all these acquisitions should be acquired through proper and fair means and kept within reasonable limits. The wealth and other means so acquired must be put to right and healthy use. These should not be wasted in ostentation or for displaying false pride. Material knowledge and wealth acquired by following the material path should be utilized for purpose of charity and for providing services to the society for public welfare.

In the material path of life, let us see, what do we actually do? All our efforts are concentrated mainly on earning more and more money. If we earn in hundreds a month we want to earn in thousands, and if we earn in thousands we wish to earn in lakhs and millions and so on. There is perhaps no limit to man's greed for wealth. And what do we do with that wealth. Besides storing money in bags and banks, we spend it in various ways. We spend lots of money in the fulfilment of our worldly desires. It may be relevant to quote here a few lines from the famous English poet, William Wordsworth:-

'World is too much with us, getting and spending, we lay waste our powers.'

We spend this wealth in purchasing goodies of life and spend most of our life in their enjoyment. There are so many ways of spending money in more or less wasteful expenditure. While doing so, one is left with little time for spiritual pursuits.

An appropriate solution for getting out of this mess is to maintain a proper balance between the two paths. To start with one should begin with self-enquiry. The essence of spirituality lies in knowing the reality of some of the fundamental questions. Who am I? What is the real purpose of life? How should we live life. All these and some more related questions which explore truth beyond material life. Spiritual enlightenment can be attained through self-enquiry and contemplation. Other simple and practicable exercises which include daily prayer, meditation, study of good literature, practice of yogic discipline, company of spiritual persons etc can help in turning the mind engrossed in material way towards spiritual way of life. By maintaining a proper balance between the two paths, one shall gradually keep on building a reservoir of purity of mind, right thinking and goodness. And practice of good qualities and good deeds will, in due course, direct the individual self towards the path of spiritual awareness. These exercises combined with self-discipline have to be continued on a regular basis over a long period of time and may be over several births, after which self-illumination could be attained. Spiritual journey is long and arduous, but there is light at the end of the tunnel. Goodness which is the result of the purity of mind, is a sure investment which never fails.

The middle path is far less difficult than the spiritual path but much more beneficial and desirable than the material path. Most right thinking people who believe in goodness and the practice of moral values would like to follow the material path. Our transitory life on earth should not be prolonged in an unending circle of deaths and births, in which process we have to go through a vicious cycle of pleasure and pain. The middle path, therefore, should be lived in such a way that after a reasonable period of time, one automatically, switches on to the spiritual path – the human life should be meaningful and purposeful and ultimately lead to the real purpose of life. While actually living in the world it should be enjoyable, peaceful and full of happiness which is not fleeting and transitory. This can happen only when the material path and spiritual path first coalesce and then the spiritual path transcends the material path. It may be kept in mind that it is only the spiritual path that can lead to total happiness which follows when one attains close proximity with the supreme reality.

After taking the first step of self-enquiry followed by other spiritual exercises mentioned earlier, the subsequent practical approach lies in doing good in every way possible. Incase one finds difficult to do good in all walks of life and to all beings, one should first practice not to do anything bad or harmful to anybody. With gradual practice one would follow the right road to spirituality and understand the true meaning and purpose of life. When one reaches that stage there shall be no looking back and one will enjoy even crossing the hardships on the way.

Holy scriptures and our ancient traditions guide us towards the spiritual path even while moving through the material world. Human beings, therefore should not get deeply immersed all their life, in the enjoyment of worldly comforts and mundane pleasures. They should after regular introspection and self-analysis aim for the highest stage of spiritual advancement. This is possible through yogic discipline. The attraction of worldly pleasures is such that these restrain an individual and keep him tied down to a limited goal of material happiness. But when a real devotee, through gradual advancement on the spiritual path, gets a real taste of spiritual enjoyment, he then tries to pull himself up from material bondage and attachment and cuts off all his undesirable worldly connections. In conclusion of all the discussion which we had gone through so far, it follows that all human beings must seriously contemplate on the nature and effects of worldly happiness acquired by following the material path and then try to escape from its evil influence and adverse consequences. The way to eternal happiness lies in following the spiritual path of life. We should, therefore make the best use of our present state of existence by following this path whole-heartedly. Therein lies our salvation!

Practical Tips

(Yamas and Niyamas for Daily Life)

We have already mentioned very briefly about yamas and niyamas as the first two parts of Ashtang Yoga. These rules of personal and social conduct should be practiced in daily life. These are the first few essential steps to mould our life from the material to the spiritual path. It is therefore considered necessary to describe these further in some detail for proper follow-up as follows:-

The five Yamas are as mentioned below:-

Ahimsa (Non-violence.) It is generally known as non-violence, but it has a greater meaning to it. Ahimsa means without himsa or no himsa. To understand ahimsa properly, we need to know what is himsa which is generally taken as physical violence which includes body injury, hurt and killing or murder. But mere non-violence is not ahimsa – which is much more than that. Its true meaning extends beyond the physical level of violence. The translation in English of ahimsa as non-violence is therefore inadequate.

Himsa may be physical, verbal and even mental. To hurt others wilfully, with hate, anger and injustice etc. are some forms of himsa. Thus the various forms of himsa in daily acts of everyday life include killing injury and physical hurt, verbal abuse, harsh words, emotional hurt etc. Even thinking of evil or having ill will or hatred or enmity against others is himsa. Abusing, cursing reacting bodily with bad intentions, displaying resentment and anger are also some of the minor forms of himsa.

The opposite of Himsa is Ahimsa.

In other words, to treat all beings with love and without anger, hatred and injustice is Ahimsa. As hatred can not remove hated, only love can win over hatred, jealousy and animosity. Ahimsa can be achieved in three forms, with mind, speech and body. It has to be practiced in word, thought and deed. Ahimsa involves complete elimination of evil thoughts and enmity of all types. Ahimsa is linked with peace and progress and is relevant even in war. Red cross and other humanitarian activities of non-violent nature play their useful role in wars. Love, fearlessness, mental restraint and discipline, equal-mindedness, fellow-feeling desire for peace, pity, sympathy etc are some of the basis of ahimsa. While talking of ahimsa we should also know and understand the reasons leading to himsa. These reasons or causes may be divided into the following two types:-

Internal – These are mental and emotional in nature and include hatred, jealousy, dislike, anger, absence of internal peace, intolerance, impatience, lack of restraint violence in mind etc.

External – These belong to the external world and include poverty, hunger, injustice, religious and social differences, political factors, greed, inequality in social religious and community level etc.

It is essential to remove these causes in order to promote Ahimsa or non-violence.

As a general rule, it is desirable to practice and promote Ahimsa in most situations. However, one may have no option but to resort to himsa in certain specific situations such as in war and in self-defense etc. One is bound to kill small harmful creatures, insects, ants etc. while walking or doing household chores or professional jobs etc. There are living organism in plants and vegetables, milk, curd and other fermented foods and drinks etc, which one has to consume. Soldiers have to fight and kill the enemy. The police have to fight, punish and even kill anti-social elements wherever necessary. The law has to hang and kill murderers. Sometime a person has to kill a thief or a robber in self-defiance or for own safety and protection. Harmful insects in home like cockroaches, mosquitoes etc have to be killed to prevent diseases. Parents and teachers have to punish naughty children. Thus himsa has to be resorted to in such and similar other situations. The general rule, therefore may be to abstain from unnecessary, undesirable and uncalled for himsa. At the same time, ahimsa may not be practiced in such a way that it becomes a weakness and cowardice. In this context, Mahatma Gandhi, one of the greatest promoters of ahimsa expressed his views as follows:-

'I would have India resort to arms in order to defend her honour than that she should in a cowardly manner become or remain a helpless victim to her dishonour.'

How to Practice Ahimsa

First of all, one must understand the concept, think over it and realize the adverse consequences of himsa. When one fully understands it, he will surely give up and avoid himsa. The basis of ahimsa is the thought process. The attitude of ahimsa has to be ingrained in the mind. Any thought of himsa has to be crushed. One must put oneself in the situation of the victim of himsa and try to feel its hurtful and dangerous consequences,

The thought of ones own suffering and realization of its evil effects will make one not to indulge in himsa. The inculcation of this spirit will pave the way to ahimsa.

Another sure way to follow ahimsa is to keep God always in mind, remember HIM and consider whether He would approve any violent thought or act. One should remember God as the creator of all beings. This thought will create fellow feeling of love and regard for others. As ahimsa should be practiced in word, thought and deed it has to he practiced in daily life in varying situations as far as possible. The attitude of ahimsa should be observed with reference to not only the other fellow human beings, but also with other living creatures which include birds, animals harmless insects, plant life and general environment as far as possible.

It should be our duty to practice ahimsa in daily life. We can do this in the following ways:-

1. Speak gently and walk carefully.
2. Think positive.
3. Respect the views of others. Do not thrust your opinion on unwilling recipients.
4. Avoid abusive foul language.
5. Exercise control over anger.
6. Do not gather evil thoughts and bad feelings in your mind.
7. Do not cause physical injury or hurt other living beings.

8. Do not kill unless it is unavoidable.
9. Avoid meat eating, drinking and smoking.
10. Follow the proverb do unto others as you wish to be done by.

An attitude of non-violence (ahimsa) should prevail in all situations as far as possible.

Satya (Truth)

This is the second Yama.

The meaning of Sanskrit word Satya (सत्य) is Truth. It also means that which exists and that which is reality. It also implies that which exists always and remains the same. Satya has a spiritual significance. That is why the saying – God is Truth or Truth is God. God is the highest truth. Satya has following three main features:

1. It always remains the same, in past, present and future.
2. It represents right knowledge.
3. It stands for general welfare. Truth prevails.

It is also said that there is no religion nobler than truth and no sin worse than untruth.

Now let us consider the implication and application of truth in daily life. An Indian saint and reformer has said "To speak and write of a thing and to believe it to be so as it really is – this is truth". Thus in real life, one should first establish the reality, then accept and believe it and thereafter follow in action, in accordance with the correct knowledge and belief. The established reality of truth should be put into practice, in thought, word and deed. One should not think, speak and act differently to suit various purposes. The reality of truth can be established on the basis of observation, inference and authority. The knowledge, speech and action contrary to truth is untruth.

As a general rule, all people should speak the truth at all times, keeping general welfare in mind. However, truth should not be used to insult, to hurt or to harm others intentionally. For speaking the truth, thoughts have to be true. Some people say something which is different from what they actually think. This amounts to untruth or falsehood. Again some people say something and do something else. There is no similarity between speech and action. This is also untruth and false conduct or hypocrisy. Truth must be the same is thought, speech and action. True thinking, speech and action are interconnected.

Some Exceptions to the Rule

The general rule is – always speak the truth.

It would appear that there are certain situations in which, it would not be advisable to speak the truth in the interest or the welfare of the people or for a good cause. Some examples are given below:

You need not call a blind or a lame person blind or lame so that it hurts his feelings, unnecessarily. Calling an aged person as an old (which he really is) is also undesirable.

Similar is the case for an ugly looking person. Truth in such cases must be tampered with sweetness and propriety. A blind man may be called brother and an old man as uncle or babuji, so that their feelings are not hurt and we shall not lose anything in doing so. Rather, we shall feel some pleasure and the other person also shall not feel unhappy. There may be some other cases also where one has to make exceptions, but such cases should be restricted to the minimum level. There is no justification for speaking untruth to serve a purely selfish, illegal and illegitimate interest. There is an instance in Mahabharata where even Dharmaraj Yudhishtra was made to resort to untruth in the interest of Dharma. But such cases should be rare.

In everyday real life, we resort to untruth in several ways. Some of us are professional liers because of the profession they fellow. Lying has become routine in some professions. Thus salesperson, some shopkeepers etc. generally hide the truth and lie to sell their goods. Some lawyers not only lie themselves but also recommend it to their clients in order to win a case. Some doctors also do when they give false hopes and console their patients by distorting facts and so on. Sometimes parents lie to their children to hide some facts or in certain situations when they think that lying may do them good. Friends, classmates, fellowworkers and neighbours live to each other to suit their selfish ends. This list is so long that, perhaps, there may be some rare beings who can be left out!

In the above sad scenario, let us consider how we can practice truth in daily life.

Practice of Truth in Daily Life

As a General Rule, truth should be spoken by all, at all times and in all the ways i.e. in thought, speech and action. One of the commandments of the Christian Faith says, 'Thou shall not lie.' In vedic view 'truth always wins'. Similarly in all other religions and faiths, truth occupies the highest place. However, in daily life, as mentioned before, this may not be as easy as advised by our religious philosophy. Moreover, truth in everyday life should be practiced with care and caution and right understanding of the situation prevailing. In this context, the following observations may be kept in mind:

1. Truth should be generally spoken in a manner that it does not insult, hurt or harm and without intentions. Exceptions have to be made here and there.
2. Truth should be tampered with sweetness.
3. Truth should lead to common welfare.
4. Truth should not be used to settle some score etc.

Asteya (Non-stealing)

This is the third yama of Ashtang Yoga.

In order to understand asteya, it is first necessary to understand steya. The meaning of steya, if loosely translated is to steal. To take away something unjustly, deceitfully or without the permission of the owner is steya and not to do so is asteya. Broadly speaking, we may say that asteya means 'non-stealing' or 'non-greed' etc. However, its real meaning extends beyond the act of mere stealing. Even harbouring the thought of acquiring something which does not belong to you is steya.

In real life, the act of stealing, snatch, robbery breaking in a house, pick-pocketing, taking a bribe, any form of corruption, fraud etc are some examples of steya. Even adulteration in foods and drinks, weighing or measuring less, cheating in examination, making false statements or giving wrong information, ticket-less travel, non-payment of loan etc. are some examples of steya in everyday life. Deceiving customers through wrong and deceptive advertisements or through false and misleading tempting promises fall in the same category. Other examples of steya include, acquisition of wealth and property to which one has no moral or legal right, accepting bribes and unauthorized commission, collecting money by floating false companies or establishments, accepting gifts for an illegal purpose, getting induce and undeserved promotion through immoral tactics, seeking admission or jobs by unfair means, collecting or buying false degrees etc. are some of the many examples of steya. Even plucking of flowers, fruits and other similar products from an orchard or a field, without the permission of their owners, are also some minor examples of steya.

The above list is not exhaustive and more cases of this type may be added to it. In nutshell, the tendency or act of having something, which does not belong to you, for yourself, physically or otherwise, without the permission of the owner and without paying proper price or through fraudulent or deceitful means is steya. The opposite of this is asteya.

In the practice of spiritual path the tendency or act of steya has to be curbed from the very beginning of such thought or intention. Parents and teachers have a big role to play in order to curb steya in their wards, from the very childhood, so that this tendency does not grow further when they become adults and follow some profession. Such evil practices must be nipped in the bud so that they do not become bad habits later on.

The practice of asteya brings contentment, happiness and self-respect and adds to one's reputation and dignity. A person who has achieved asteya will work hard and follow the dictum 'honesty is the best policy' when a person, for all times, shows this tendency in thought, word and deed, only then he is supposed to have established in asteya. Such a person becomes a true devotee of God and successfully pursues the spiritual path. In short, asteya is the very basis of honest, right-thinking, truthful living and is a sure way to Godliness.

Brahmacharya (Celibacy)

This is the fourth Yama.

In common parlance, Brahmacharya means celibacy and maintenance of strict discipline in the matter of sexual indulgence. One is a celibate when one does not marry and does not perform sexual act, at all. Such a person may be difficult to find but there have been several such examples in our history and tradition.

There is another view also, less strict and with some modification. A person may be married, has a wife but he does not associate with any other woman, in so far as his sex life is concerned. Even with his own wife, his sexual relations may be limited and strictly regulated. In such a case there has to be complete control over lust and sexual urge both in thought and deed. The ideal position here is that sexual acts are performed only for the purpose of producing a child and not for mere entertainment or to satisfy sexual desire.

There is also another interpretation of Brahmacharya, Brahma means God and Charya means conduct. Thus it means a well-regulated conduct, a way of married life or otherwise, which leads to god. It is, in fact, a self-imposed moral discipline, by itself, without any outside pressure or provocation. For a practitioner of spiritual path, it is necessary that he should maintain purity of thought, conserve his basic urges and energies, in order to direct his life purposefully towards achieving God consciousness. Safeguarding sexual energy, conserving it or sublimating it are therefore important aspects of observing brahmacharya.

It may not be practicable to follow such a strict regimen, for a common householder. For him, absolute elimination of sexual indulgence is impossible. A married person cannot be expected to be a celibate. But he is expected to exercise a reasonable self-control over his sexual urge.

There may be different standards in different stages of life.

A student and a young man who is in the process of preparation of his life, is expected to be completely celibate before marriage. A married person is expected to confine his sexual relations with his wife only. Even in doing so, he should practice restraint in acts of sexual indulgence. In an ideal case of married life, sexual acts may be resorted only to produce a child and not for mere enjoyment or for self-gratification. This is an extremely difficult goal to achieve! An ageing or a retired person has to limit his sexual desires to the minimum possible. In order to do so, he should keep busy in the pursuit of spiritual knowledge or involve himself in acts of social service etc. A hermit or a sanyasi or a spiritual saint is expected to be beyond any type of sexual gratification even in thought or imagination.

The observance of Brahmacharya enables a person to achieve control over the mind and the body. It is a means for the acquisition of true knowledge and enables practitioners to follow the spiritual path successfully. By preserving the vital sexual energy, one can maintain the strength of the body and the mind. Regular worship of God, prayer and mediation, right food, physical exercises, reading of good literature and good company observance of good conduct and moral values etc are some of the effective means to achieve Brahmacharya which should be observed in thought, word and deed.

Brahmacharya can prove a great asset in the gradual progress on the spiritual path.

Aparigraha (Non-greed or Non-accumulation of Material Possessions)

This is the last Yama.

In order to understand aparigraha, one must first understand parigraha.

The general meaning of parigraha is to acquire, to possess, to procure, to accumulate, to gain etc.

One can acquire wealth, property and other material possessions. Both need and greed are the basis of parigraha.

Aparigraha is the opposite of parigraha. To acquire, possess and hoard all material things which are unnecessary and in excess of actual requirements is called parigraha and not to do so is aparigraha. It implies not only giving up of all these things but also not to have even the desire for such possessions. Parigraha indicates greed while aparigraha stands for sacrifice.

It is natural for a householder to acquire wealth and property in order to maintain a household but there should be a limit to these acquisitions. Our genuine needs must be fulfilled but desires should not become our needs. It is unnecessary and not advisable to acquire wealth and property in excess of actual requirements. If one small house is enough for a family, it is not desirable to acquire a big mansion or an additional home. This rule should also apply to other material objects. As one desire leads to another and since desires are never satiated it is very essential to keep them within limit. One must distinguish between a genuine need and a desire. While needs may be limited, our desires may have no limit!

Man, by nature, has an instinct of acquisition. While he needs material possessions for his sustenance, preservation, and reasonable comfort, the situation becomes worse, when this tendency gives rise to vices like stealing, robberies, cunningness, jealousy, unhealthy completion, deception enmity, fights and similar other evils. Thus man's greed to have more and more can cause family fights and unsocial activities. A person caught in the web of parigraha can forsake his friends, relative, religion, community and his country. While a person may acquire material possessions and feel rich and proud, have social status etc, he can never get peace of mind which comes from contentment or aparigraha.

Aparigraha leads to non-attachment, broadmindedness, sacrifice and renunciation. Consequently, a person who practices aparigraha becomes free from pain and misery which are caused by the loss of material possessions. In order to practice aparigraha in everyday life, one should keep in mind the following points.

1. Limit your desires.

2. Practice restraint in the use of daily requirements.

3. Minimise your other needs, such as property, jewellery, items of entertainment and pleasure etc.

4. Practice charity and help others, as much as possible.

5. Avoid the use of objects of ease and pleasure.
6. Eat to live and do not live to eat.
7. Fulfill your essential needs but do not make desires your needs.

A person who observes aparigraha is a contented person. He is a happy person without greed and unnecessary cravings and this attains peace of mind. Such a person is well on the spiritual path and makes progress gradually.

Niyamas

The niyamas, which are also five in number form the second part of Ashtang Yoga. These are the means of personal discipline and tell us how to interact with ourselves. The five niyamas are as follows:

1. Shaucha (Cleanliness)
2. Santosha (Contentment)
3. Tapa (Austesity)
4. Swadhyay (Study of scriptures and other good literature)
5. Ishwar Pranidhan (Surrender to God)

Shaucha (Cleanliness)

This is the first of the five niyamas. It is of two types – internal and external. External shaucha means cleanliness of the body and objects we use, including, dress, food, house and our physical environment. It also includes our conduct in professional life, especially the means of earning money and our work culture.

Regular and proper bathing, wearing clean clothes, keeping the house and its environment clean, keeping food and other household items clean etc. are some of the examples of external shaucha. There is great emphasis on the purity of food intake. This does not mean only what we eat i.e. the material stuff. It also includes thoughts and what we hear and acquire from outside. While external shaucha is very important, it is less consequential than the inner shaucha or internal purity.

Internal shaucha means purity of mind, intellect, thoughts and feelings, heart and soul. While it may be easier to keep our body and external objects clean, it is lot more difficult to maintain internal purity. One has to first get rid of impure thoughts and feelings. All negative thoughts and feelings have to be avoided. Internal shaucha therefore involves removal of ignorance, attachment, lust, greed, anger, false pride and similar other evils etc.

The observance of shaucha purifies body, mind and intellect. Accordingly, through shaucha, one develops right conduct and cheerful pure mind. The purity of mind is utmost essential for the spiritual path of life. A pure and cheerful mind has better concentration which enables a devotee to focus better on the path of God-realisation.

Santosha (Contentment)

Broadly speaking, Santosha means the absence of desire to process more of the necessities of life than are necessary for its preservation. It implies that one should work honestly to one's full capacity and capability and be satisfied with the result of his efforts, whatever it may be.

Contentment is a state of mind. It is the inner mental poise and does not depend upon external circumstances and influences. However, it does not imply passivity. It is also wrong to believe that contentment will follow, if desires are fulfilled, as desires are never satiated. It also does not mean that a person should do nothing to achieve progress in life or withdraw himself from society or become a recluse. It also does not mean that one should accept whatever is available to him with a sense of fatality and this should not try to better his lot. It really means making all efforts and then be satisfied with what you get. There should be no anger or disappointment, grief or unhappiness if the result is not in proportion to the efforts made or is contrary to the expectations.

Contentment does not evolve all of a sudden. One has to develop an attitude on a gradual and continuous basis. In our life, we have to get along with patience and courage, without fun or frustration, self-pity or depression. One need not be flustered with success or unduly bother over failure. All happenings should be taken in one's stride, in an unmitigated and unruffled calm manner. The mental poise or the equanimity of mind thus established will lead to contentment.

The attitude of contentment develops a cheerful mind. It elevates a person above selfish limitations giving him peace and moral strength. It is the seed for spiritual delights, a positive condition for perpetual joy of existence. Contentment strengthens our faith in God. It gives a realization that all the pleasures of the world are temporary. It weakens and ultimately extinguishes man's craving for more and more fulfilment of one's desires. It acts as a source of internal peace and builds up the stamina. One sure method to attain contentment is to engage the mind in constant meditation of God.

In short, contentment is a glad acceptance of what comes to us by circumstance or by providence, in spite of our best efforts. It is the greatest wealth. Therefore, one should always try to observe contentment in all possible manner.

Tapa (Austerity)

It is the capacity or practice to face all odds in the performance of one's Dharma (righteousness). Tapa implies that one should have the strength and fortitude to remain unaffected by the opposites of life, such as heat and cold, hunger and thirst, loss and gain honour and dishonor and other discomforts and obstacles which confront us in everyday life. To face all these difficulties bravely and cheerfully is Tapa. On the positive side, to cultivate virtues like the observance of truth, righteousness, tolerance, swadhyay, etc are examples of tapa. In short, the practice of good conduct in the face of all difficulties in tapa. Some ignorant persons believe that torturing the body through some funny strange harmful rituals is tapa. This is a mistaken belief. Thus sitting under the hot sun during peak summer surrounded by fire, or standing in ice cold water in winter, lying on a bed of thorns or nails and such other gimmicks do not mean tapa. It does not imply willing infliction of pain in the body.

The purifies of tapa is to build and accumulate energy and not to waste it by performing harmful rituals. What is required is to cultivate and maintain a regular discipline of life for a pure and purposeful objective. Meditation or sadhna in the true spirit is tapa.

Tapa purifies the body, mind and soul and builds their strength. Through tapa, one can control desires, senses and the mind. Tapa makes a person fearless and full of determination. With the practice of tapa, one can not only achieve desirable worldly objectives, but also can attain success in the spiritual path.

Some examples of practicing tapa in daily life may be mentioned as follows:

1. Observance of brahmacharya or control over sexual urges and their proper regulation.

2. To perform one's duty in the face of difficulties.

3. To keep away evil thoughts and to nurture good thoughts.

4. To restrict worldly desires.
5. To acquire true knowledge through swadhyaya and good company.
6. To maintain virtuous and pious conduct in all walks of life.
7. To renounce comforts and avoid temptations, as far as possible.
8. To practice pranayam and meditation.
9. To maintain proper control over food and drinks and not to have craving for tasty impure and harmful foods and drinks.
10. To have full control over lust, anger, greed and such other sinful habits.

Swadhyaya (Study of Scriptures or Good Literature)

Swadhyaya is one of the most important means to follow the spiritual path.

In common vocabulary, it means the study of the scriptures, religious books and good literature. In general, study of good literature which guides a person towards moral values, good conduct or righteousness may be deemed as swadhyaya. It may also mean study of the self or self-analysis, which involves appraisal of oneself, thinking about positive and negative tendencies and by doing so, bring about moral development and progress towards spiritual life.

Swadhyaya, however, does not mean mere reading or reading of any book or reading only for fun and entertainment or just as a pastime. It also does not mean reading only for getting information about the material world, business or profession. Even mere reading or parrot-like recitation of some religious book is not swadhyaya. One has to study carefully, properly understand the contents and put the knowledge so acquired into actual practice in real life situations, personal conduct and total behaviour. One should reflect over what has been studied and understand the correct and complete meaning of it and then use it in real life.

Swadhyaya is in the nature of self-education. One can learn from the living teachers and guides or from their works. Contact with the learned, the spiritual teacher's guides and thinkers provide excellent opportunities for self-education. While we can no longer meet the saints or the holy persons who are now no more, we can certainly study their books. In this way, we can come in contact with their thoughts and teachings, through holy scriptures and other relevant literature which contains spiritual knowledge and true wisdom. Repeated and regular study of such literature inspires, guides and improves human thoughts and actions. We have to understand rightly, assimilate the essence and then translate this knowledge into good actions. Swadhyaya requires long and sustained study and correct understanding of what has been said or written by great thinkers. It helps build the power of concentration. One is also engaged in a good mental activity. In this way both senses and mind are kept busy and under control and the mind does not become an idle workshop.

Swadhyaya helps in removing doubts and ignorance. It can also provide solutions to the problems of life. Gandhiji, found solace and solutions to his problems through the study of the Gita. If you read something good, holy and pure in the morning, it will have beneficial effect throughout the day. A sacred book like the Gita, or some other holy scripture, should be ready daily in a systematic manner. It may be useful to record the synopsis of such reading in a notebook for ready reference, later on. For the purpose of swadhyaya, only those books should be read which uplift the mind. These include scriptures, biographies of saints and great persons and their works and similar other ethical good literature.

Swadhyaya enhances true knowledge, right understanding, wisdom and purifies the mind. As pure, wholesome and nourishing food is essential for the body, swadhyaya is beneficial for the progress of the mind and the soul. It acts like a healthy tonic for the mind. According to Maharishi Patanjali, Swadhyaya can lead to divine experience. As it acts like a mental and spiritual tonic, it should be practiced daily, as long and as far as possible. It is a very useful means to attain progress in the spiritual path of life.

Ishwar Pranidhan (Surrender to God)

This is the last of the five niyamas.

It means total dedication of all our actions to the Supreme. And implies absolute faith in God, accompanied by complete and pure devotion. It involves complete resignation to the will of God. One has to first understand the true concept of God, his nature and attributes and accept HIM as Guru and Guide. It includes true worship of God and dedication of all thoughts and actions to HIM, with full faith, love and devotion.

The first step of Ishwar Pranidhan is full acceptance followed by love and adoration and total surrender, not out of fear but out of love and devotion. Heartfelt adoration of God is higher than ritual worship. It is something deeper, spontaneous, flowing from the heart.

While performing different actions of life, we need the support, guidance from our friends, relatives, colleagues etc. Thus as a child, one depends upon parents and relatives. In school, we seek help from teachers and so on. Similarly, in other walks of life, we depend upon someone or the other, in some way or the other. On a broader prospective of life, we have to seek guidance and support of God and Ishwar Pranidhan is the means to get that support.

A person who regularly practices Ishwar Pranidhan achieves a stage when he experiences love and grace of God. His ignorance is destroyed and worldly attractions like attachment, greed, ego etc whither away from his life. All other happenings of life do not disturb him and he attains peace of mind, happiness and ultimately, eternal bliss (Ananda).

Yamas and Niyamas, both combined constitute personal and social aspects of good conduct. These are to be practiced individually, as well as, in relation to society. They present a complete package of personal, social and spiritual discipline which leads to desirable conduct. Yamas and Niyams are first and second stages of Asthang Yoga and these lay the firm foundation of spiritual path of life. The worship of God will become a mere ritual without the observance of these rules and regulations in the conduct of real life.

Law for the Layman

Once a SANYASI (holy man) was delivering a sermon to a large audience. As usual he was telling them to follow the spiritual path of life in order to gain liberation from pain and misery of worldly life. For achieving this goal he told the audience, various means of spiritual discipline which were arduous and difficult to practice by an average person. As he was emphasising again and again on these difficult exercises, a young man from the audience stood up and said 'Swami Ji. All these means which you are asking us to follow are beyond our capability. Therefore please tell us something simple and easy to practice. Swami Ji thought for a while and said O.K. I shall now tell you about three simple means to live life well and happily. These are, briefly as follows:-

1. Keep Healthy

Health has been described as the greatest wealth. A healthy person can produce wealth by dint of his hard work but a sick rich man can not purchase good health simply by means of his wealth. Good health is utmost essential for performing various actions of daily life successfully. One should, therefore, follow rules of good health and take all necessary steps to keep healthy. This is the first step towards living life well and happily. Both body and mind should be kept healthy in all possible and desirable manners.

2. Keep Busy

Life has to be full of actions. Life without action means death. One must therefore, keep busy in some useful activity and follow the saying – an empty mind is the devils' workshop. Apart from one's, professional work and daily duties one should use ones spare time in some healthy and beneficial pursuit, a constructive hobby, social service, reading and writing, meditation and prayer, music and sport etc. One should plan and execute ones actions with dedication and whole-heartedness. While keeping busy, one has to love what one is doing. It will give you confidence and the determination to face all odds and ultimately attain success and happiness, of course, all our actions to keep busy should be based on righteousness and for general welfare. This will give us a feeling of goodness within and it will make our life good and happy. Keep working as work is the basic necessity of life. But one should put both head and heart into work so that it becomes simple and efficient and not boring. Remember the dictum work is worship. Life will become well-adjusted and cheerful if we make work true worship.

3. Remain Carefree

Life becomes simple, efficient and cheerful if we develop a carefree attitude. We often worry about ups and downs, deficiencies and defects, needs and necessities, failures and defeats and several similar other factors where things do not go the way we want. It such undesirable situations, we do worry very often. The right thing is to learn to reconcile to the situation and try to find a way out. We need not be disturbed or disheartened and face the crisis with courage. A care free attitude does not mean that one need not plan ahead and make suitable efforts to ward off any unsavory situation that may lie ahead. One sure way to cultivate carefree attitude is to do one's best and leave the rest to God. Self-confidence and full faith and confidence in God are the keys to develop a carefree attitude in life. When we live our life in a spirit of total surrender to the supreme power all our cases and worries of life will be taken care of by HIM. An unswerving deep faith in God accompanied by righteous actions will enable us to inculcate a carefree attitude. This will make our living worthy, happy and cheerful. The above discussion about three simple means to live life as advised by the holy man, is somewhat expanded version of what he really said. In fact, he spoke only three words in Hindi which are as follow:-

स्वस्थ रहो, व्यस्त रहो, मस्त रहो।

In English, there words may be translated as follows:-

Keep Healthy, Keep Busy, Remain Carefree.

Apparently, this is a simple formula to live life well and happily as it does not involve any intricate and arduous exercises of strict religious discipline. It may not be as easy or simple as it looks to practice this formula but one can try make efforts and see the result. An average person can simply try to work it out. So always remember these three words, try to practice in real life and leave the rest to God who will surely reward your efforts.

Epilogue

Everyone in this world wants to be happy. Happiness is thus the most-wanted commodity in human life. Various people seek and get happiness in numerous ways. Broadly speaking happiness may be categorized under two sub-heads – material and spiritual – material happiness is the most popular brand while spiritual happiness is sought and attained by the rarest of the rare persons. Material happiness is attained through material means by the contact of the senses with the sense objects. We taste and eat delicious foods, see pleasant objects and rights, hear sweet songs and voices, touch soft and soothing objects and smell sweet and pleasant odours and so on. Similar examples can be multiplied. All these material things and activities provide us pleasure and sensual happiness. However there are some serious drawbacks which accompany such happiness. First of all it produces attachment which becomes the cause of bondage leading to pain and miseries of worldly life. Then this type of happiness is short-lived and is often accompanied by pain or followed by it. All these material comforts and pleasures are obtained through money. It is said that money can buy anything. In order to get material happiness the pursuit of acquisition of wealth becomes the main objective of life. A person desirous of material happiness becomes a prey to various evils which include greed, lust, false pride, anger, ignorance and so on. In this process he remains entangled in the vicious cycle of pleasure and pain and other dualities of life. This leads to a chain of numerous births and deaths resulting in perpetual bondage and miseries of human life. This is not a desirable objective of life.

The spiritual happiness stands on a different footing. It results from the constant practice of yogic discipline which is a synthesis of righteous actions, right knowledge and understanding, full faith and devotion in the supreme spirit. Unlike material path, the spiritual path is full of obstacles and severe hardships which have to be overcome before the eternal bliss is attained. In this path, it is essential to purify one's mind and soul and get rid of all evil tendencies such as, lust, greed, anger, false pride, jealousy attachment and ignorance. A pure life of righteous actions without attachment is a pre-requisite for living a spiritual life. It is extremely difficult to follow this path amidst all sorts of worldly allurements and temptations. It is said that the material happiness tastes sweet and gives pleasure to start with but its end result is bitter and painful. The case of spiritual path is just the reverse of it. It is bitter and painful to begin with but after one gains the highest knowledge, the result is sweet and full of bliss. It is relevant to quote here a verse from the Upanishad as follows:-

The face of Truth (Reality) is covered with a golden lid. Uncover that reality with devotion. The material path is like the golden lid which obstructs the view of the reality. In order to know the reality, one has to uncover the lid, by following the spiritual path. Both the paths can lead to happiness, as indicated in the following verse from the Vedas:-

"Thou shall find the desired happiness arising from the contact of the objects with the senses by performing with the body righteous works, with attachment. Thou shall attain emancipation (highest happiness) by performing actions without attachment."

The happiness attained through material path is sensual and hence temporary and is accompanied by pain and misery. The happiness attained through spiritual path, without any attachment, is eternal – free from any pain and bondage. Thus two types of happiness can be attained by following two different paths, material and spiritual. Both the paths are before you – which way to follow – the choice lies with you. In this context the following verse from the Veda can help you to make your choice–

> Rise above material desires
>
> To the heavenly path of spiritual experience
>
> And behold the light divine
>
> Guiding these towards eternal joy

Yajurveda – 8.52